CONTENTS

Countdown to Calamity, or Hope for the Future?

*Current events in
the light of
Bible prophecy*

Tony Pearce

New Wine Press

New Wine Ministries
PO Box 17
Chichester
West Sussex
United Kingdom
PO19 2AW

ISBN 978-1-905991-64-8

Typeset by **documen**, www.documen.co.uk
Cover design by CCD, www.ccdgroup.co.uk
Printed in the United Kingdom

1 *Countdown to Calamity?*

IIIIIIIIIIIIIIIIIIIIIIIIIIIIIIIIIIIIIIIIIIIIIIIIIIIIIIIIIIIIIIIIIIIIIIIIIIIIIIIIIIIIIIIIIIIIIIIIIIIIIIIIIIIIIIIIIIIIIIIIIIIIIIIIIIII

Many people are waking up to the fact that the world really is threatened with disaster on multiple fronts – the spread of weapons of mass destruction, the threat of economic collapse, the dependency of the world system on oil which will run out, the environmental issue, the Middle East conflict, violence and lawlessness abounding, breakdown of family life and the resulting insecurity facing millions. All these lead people to ask 'Is the world as we know it coming to an end?'

The fact that I am writing this book and you are reading it shows that it is not quite the end yet, but it is remarkable how many things are happening which make people wonder whether this is the way the world is heading.

Hollywood has picked up on this with a number of disaster films being produced. *The Wall Street Journal* (31/7/09) carried an article 'Hollywood Destroys The World':

> *'A flood of post apocalyptic stories is now headed toward movie theatres and TV screens. Director Roland Emmerich has nearly destroyed the world three times already. This time, he means to finish the job. In his next movie, 2012, which comes out in November, the earth will rip apart, fulfilling an ancient prophecy.'*

The article goes on to list a number of coming films about a future calamity destroying civilisation and how a handful of people remain to scratch around a ruined world for survival – *The Book of Eli, Day One, The Colony*, and *The Road*. Giving a reason for this it says, 'Most of the storytellers say they are reacting to anxiety over real threats in uncertain times: the terrorist attacks of September 11, 2001, two US wars abroad, multiple pandemics, a global financial crisis and new attention to environmental perils.'

Roland Emmerich's film *2012* asks the question: 'How would the governments of our planet prepare six billion people for the end of the world?' Its answer: 'They wouldn't.' The film *2012* is based on the fact that the Mayan 'Long Count' Calendar ends on December 21st, 2012. According to some interpretations of what this means, the gods will bring an end to human life and start again with new creatures.

Type in '2012' in an Internet search engine and you will find thousands of websites announcing a coming calamity on that date. One scenario for this happening is that the alignment of the earth with the sun and the centre of the Milky Way Galaxy, scheduled to occur in 2012, releases massive energy and heats up the earth's core, causing earthquakes, volcanoes and tsunamis world-wide.

NASA has warned about the possibility of a massive increase in solar activity causing a geomagnetic storm in 2013, which could paralyse the planet. High radiation levels from massive solar flares resulting in a geomagnetic storm would knock out satellites, power grids, air travel, GPS navigation and radio communications. It would cause world-wide blackouts and cripple the internet for weeks or even months, with disastrous knock-on effects on both the world economy and the lives of ordinary people.

The UN's IPCC (Intergovernmental Panel on Climate Change) claims that global warming caused by burning carbon will cause calamitous climate change unless urgent measures are taken to stop it. Polar ice will melt, sea levels will rise, low lying islands and coastal areas will be flooded, including major cities like London, New York and Shanghai. There will be droughts in some places and floods in others. Opening ceremonies at the Copenhagen Climate Change Conference in December 2009 began with a short film featuring children of the future facing an apocalypse of tempests and desert landscapes, if world leaders failed to act. "Please help save the world", said a little girl, plaintively, as the waters rose around the tree she was clinging onto.

Others are prophesying financial Armageddon as the massive debts left behind by the financial crisis of 2008 cause a second wave of financial meltdown leading to the collapse of the world economy. Another potential crisis is that energy shortages cause the lights to go out and the system that depends on the constant supply of electricity and oil crashes. Or a virus will rage out of control and kill millions, as was portrayed on the BBC's TV series 'Survivors'. Or cyber-terrorists will knock out the world's computer systems or shut down the electricity generating system. Or maybe terrorists will unleash mass destruction with a dirty bomb attack on London or New York.

In the US there is fear of what would happen in the event of an EMP (Electromagnetic Pulse) attack that would knock out the country's power grid in a second. A device fired from a ship off the coast of America could detonate a crude nuclear weapon above the earth and knock out communication systems, electric power, transportation, water, food and other infrastructure. As a result America would be plunged back into the dark ages. No wonder books are circulating with titles like *How to survive the collapse of civilization*.

An Internet advertisement for this book asks:

What if the unthinkable happened? Could your family survive, even for a few weeks, without electricity, hospitals, water pumped in from miles away and food trucked in from out of state? If terrorists succeed in attacking the US power grid with an electromagnetic pulse (EMP) device, they could throw America into the dark ages in a split second. Find out what you can do to prepare to survive a terrorist strike, global epidemic, social unrest, or other serious disasters.

Both sides of the Middle East conflict see potential apocalyptic events around the corner. The Rabbinic Council of Judea and Samaria issued a statement in June 2010 that we are now in 'the beginning of the Gog and Magog process where the world is against us, but which ends with the third and final redemption'. In this they are referring to the biblical prophecy found in Ezekiel 38-39 of the last days' battle in which God rescues Israel from an invasion of hostile nations.

From the other side of the conflict Iran's Ayatollah Khamenei has called on Muslim nations around the world to unite militarily in response to the imminent coming of Islam's messianic saviour – the Mahdi. Political and religious leaders in Iran have made statements that we are in the last days of this age and that, following a time of great conflict on earth, the Mahdi will usher in the end of the age, causing the Muslims to defeat Israel and the West and rule the world.

All these different views may be interesting, but there is one source of information which has contained prophecies of a time like ours coming for thousands of years – the Bible. Today most people are being conditioned to disbelieve and ignore this source, but it is the only one which can really offer us any light at the end of the tunnel. In fact it offers us light while we are in the tunnel as well!

Every month I produce a talk on 'This month in Prophecy' and a column in the magazine *Prophetic Witness* called 'Signs of the Times'. These contain events which have happened in the previous month and line up with Bible prophecies of the last days and the Second Coming of Jesus Christ. As I look at all the material before me I have to conclude that the human race is heading for calamitous events which line up with the Bible prophecies of the Great Tribulation.

Jesus spoke of this in Matthew 24:21-22:

> *'For then there will be great tribulation, such as has not been since the beginning of the world until this time, no nor ever shall be. And unless those days were shortened, no flesh would be saved; but for the elect's sake those days will be shortened.'*

This means that there will be such a calamity on the earth that if God did not cut short these days it would mean the end of life on earth. This prophecy also implies that God will not allow this period to go on to the point where all life is extinguished.

A number of Old Testament passages also focus on the time of great trouble in the period at the end of this age. Isaiah 24 describes the last days' crisis:

> *'Behold the LORD makes the earth empty and makes it waste, distorts its surface and scatters abroad its inhabitants. The earth mourns and fades away, the world languishes and fades away; the haughty people of the earth languish. The earth is also defiled under its inhabitants, because they have transgressed the laws, changed the ordinance, broken the everlasting*

covenant. Therefore the curse has devoured the earth,
and those who dwell in it are desolate. Therefore
the inhabitants of the earth are burned, and few men
are left.

(Isaiah 24:1-6)

In the Book of Revelation we read of a number of disasters striking the earth which tie in with current world problems. World wars and famines cause mass death (Revelation 6:1-8). Trees and the grass are burned up, the fish of the sea die as something like a great mountain is thrown into the sea (asteroid?) and fresh waters become undrinkable (Revelation 8:7-11). A dictatorship arises which forces people to accept a mark and a number (666) without which you cannot buy or sell (Revelation 13). Rivers dry up and people are scorched with great heat (Revelation 16). The final battle of Armageddon brings the armies of the world together in Israel and closes this age with the physical return of the Lord Jesus Christ to the earth (Revelation 16:16, 19:11-21).

The Bible also gives us a great hope in the physical Second Coming of the Lord Jesus Christ and the deliverance of all those who accept Him as Saviour and Lord. The disaster movies end with either no survivors or a handful of survivors scratching around in a dying planet. In the Bible the catastrophic events of the last days will be followed by the physical return of the Lord Jesus with all those who have put their trust in Him. The survivors of the Great Tribulation who accept Jesus as Saviour will live in a restored earth during the 1000 year Millennium in which time Satan will be bound and unable to deceive the nations (Revelation 20) and there will be universal peace (Isaiah 2:1-4) and harmony in the natural world (Isaiah 11). This will be a prelude to eternity when God will create new heavens and a new earth in which righteousness dwells (2 Peter 3:13).

Concerning the events of the last days of this age Jesus said:

'When these things begin to happen, look up and lift up your heads because your redemption draws near.'

(Luke 21:28)

For the believer there is the hope of the return of Jesus Christ which we will look at in this book.

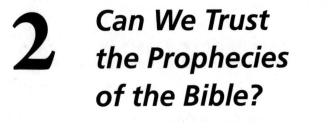

Can We Trust the Prophecies of the Bible?

Jesus promised that He would return. He told the disciples:

> '*I go to prepare a place for you and if I go and prepare a place for you, I will come again and receive you to Myself, and where I am there you may be also.*'
>
> (John 14:2-3)

When Jesus ascended into heaven from the Mount of Olives, two men (angels) told the disciples:

> '*This same Jesus who was taken up from you into heaven will so come in like manner as you saw Him go into heaven.*'
>
> (Acts 1:11)

In his letter to Titus, Paul wrote:

> '*We should live soberly, righteously and godly in the present age, looking for the blessed hope and glorious appearing of our great God and Saviour Jesus Christ.*'
>
> (Titus 2:12-13)

The Bible is full of prophecy. Over a quarter of its verses contain prophecy, as this table shows.

Total verses in the Bible	31124
Total predictions in OT	1239
OT verses containing predictions	6641 out of 23210
% of OT that is prophecy	28.5%
Total predictions in NT	578
NT verses containing predictions	1711 out of 7914
% of NT that is prophecy	21.5%
Total Prophetic topics in Bible	737
Total % of Bible that is prophecy	27%

The Bible also claims that its prophetic content is accurate and inspired by God. Peter wrote:

'We have the prophetic word confirmed which you do well to heed as a light that shines in a dark place. ... No prophecy of Scripture is of any private interpretation for prophecy never came by the will of man, but holy men of God spoke as they were moved by God.'

(2 Peter 2:19-21)

Paul wrote:

'All Scripture is given by inspiration of God and is profitable for doctrine, for reproof, for correction, for instruction in righteousness.'

(2 Timothy 3:16)

In saying this Paul must have included the parts of the Bible which have to do with prophecy.

What is the Bible's track record for fulfilment of prophecy?

Some of the prophecies of the Bible have already been fulfilled; some are in the process of happening now; and some have not yet been fulfilled. By looking at the prophecies which have already happened, and seeing their fulfilment, we can have confidence that the ones which have not yet happened will be fulfilled.

Many prophecies in the Old Testament relate to the history of Israel, both the land and the people. God told Abraham about the future of his descendants, their captivity in Egypt, the Exodus and the fact that his descendants would be as countless as the stars in the heavens and that these descendants would inherit the land of Canaan / Israel (Genesis 15). Through Moses God told the people of Israel that they would be blessed and fruitful in the land and protected from their enemies if they worshipped Him and obeyed His commands, but that they would experience His judgement if they were disobedient and worshipped idols. The final judgement for disobedience would be removal from the land (Leviticus 26, Deuteronomy 28). However even if they are removed they will return because of the covenant made with Abraham. The rest of the Hebrew Bible shows how these prophecies worked out in the history of Israel.

Many prophecies were very specific. Isaiah prophesied the captivity of Israel in Babylon a century and a half before it happened. Jeremiah who lived in the generation that saw the exile happen prophesied that this period of exile would last 70 years:

> 'For thus says the Lord: "After seventy years are
> completed in Babylon I will visit you and perform

My good word to you and cause you to return to this place (Jerusalem)." '

(Jeremiah 29:10)

The exile began in the fourth year of the reign of King Jehoiakim (605/04BC) and ended with the decree of Cyrus in 536/5 BC. In his prophecy of the captivity Isaiah named the Persian King Cyrus as the one who would then conquer Babylon and make the decree that would cause the return from exile to the land of Israel. This decree was passed in approximately 536BC:

'Thus says the Lord ... Who says of Cyrus, "He is my shepherd and he shall perform all My pleasure, saying to Jerusalem, "You shall be built" and to the temple, "Your foundation shall be laid." '

(Isaiah 44:28)

The Book of Ezra opens with the decree of Cyrus for the Israelites to go back to Jerusalem from Babylon and rebuild the Temple.

As one of the Israelite captives in Babylon, Daniel received a prophecy about the rebuilding of the Temple and the walls of Jerusalem in troublesome times. The prophecy went on to say that Messiah would come during the time of the second Temple (i.e. the Temple that was rebuilt on the site of the first Temple built in Solomon's time). He would be cut off (die a violent death) not for Himself (not for His own sins but for the sins of others) before this Temple was destroyed:

'Messiah shall be cut off but not for Himself and the people of the prince to come shall destroy the city and the sanctuary.'

(Daniel 9:26)

Right on time, Jesus came as the Messiah and died a violent death (was cut off) for the sins of the world. Forty years later, as He also prophesied, the Romans came and destroyed Jerusalem and the Temple. Speaking of the Temple in Jerusalem, He said:

'If you had known even you especially in this your day
the things that make for your peace! But now they are
hidden from your eyes. For the days will come upon you
when your enemies will build an embankment around
you, surround you and level you and your children within
you to the ground; and they will not leave on you one
stone upon another, because you did not know the time of
your visitation.'

(Luke 19:41-44)

When Jesus spoke of knowing 'the time of your visitation' He meant Israel knowing that He was the Messiah coming to His people. The most important prophecies in the Hebrew scriptures (Old Testament) relate to the Messiah. These are divided into two sets of prophecies – one of the Suffering Servant, who dies as a sacrifice for the sins of the world; and one of the Reigning King, who judges the world righteously and rules Israel and the nations from Jerusalem during a period of peace and justice known as the Millennium or Messianic Kingdom.

Both sets of prophecies are fulfilled in one person, Jesus the Messiah. He has come once in humility as the Saviour who died for our sins and rose again from the dead. Through His perfect sacrifice those who repent and believe in Him now receive forgiveness of sin and eternal life. The same Lord Jesus will come again in power as King of kings and Lord of lords to judge the world in righteousness. Those who accept Him now as Saviour will be saved on the coming day of judgement; those who reject Him will be lost. That is why it is so important that we decide to follow Him now.

The prophecies of the Suffering Servant have already been fulfilled in Jesus Christ (Messiah). He was to be born to a virgin (Isaiah 7:14) in Bethlehem (Micah 5:2) coming as a Son, but at the same time being the Mighty God (Isaiah 9:6-7). He preached good news with a ministry of miracles (Isaiah 61:1), taught in parables (Psalm 78:2) and was a light to the Gentiles (Isaiah 49:6). He entered Jerusalem on a donkey (Zechariah 9:9) and was greeted by the crowds with words "Hoshienu" (this means 'save us' and is written as 'Hosanna' in the New Testament), "Blessed is He who comes in the name of the Lord" (Psalm 118:25-6). He was rejected by the chief priests and leadership of Israel (Isaiah 53:3) and betrayed for 30 pieces of silver (Zechariah 11:12-13). He was tried and condemned unjustly (Isaiah 53:7-8) and put to death by crucifixion, bearing the sins of the world (Psalm 22:16, Zechariah 12:10, Isaiah 53:4-6). He was buried in a rich man's tomb (Isaiah 53:9) and rose again from the dead (Psalm 16:10-11, Isaiah 53:8-10). He ascended into heaven (Psalm 68:18) and sent His Holy Spirit to His disciples who would take His message of salvation to the ends of the earth (Isaiah 45:22-23).

The prophecies of the Reigning King will be fulfilled when Jesus returns to judge the world and rule over the nations in the Messianic kingdom. At this time He will bring an end to war and the reign of the wicked. Satan will be bound and unable to deceive the nations until the end of the 1000-year period (Revelation 20:2-3). The Lord Jesus will rule the world from the restored Jerusalem. The earth will be full of the knowledge of the Lord and even the animal kingdom will be at peace (Isaiah 2:1-4, 11-12, Zechariah 14). As the prophecies of the Suffering Servant were literally fulfilled at the first coming of Jesus, so the prophecies of the Reigning King will be fulfilled at His Second Coming.

3 *The End Times –*
Hope or Doom?

Concerning His return, Jesus said:

> *'For as in the days before the flood they were eating*
> *and drinking, marrying and giving in marriage until the*
> *day that Noah entered the ark, and did not know until*
> *the flood came and took them all away, so also will the*
> *coming of the Son of Man be. Then two men will be in*
> *the field; one will be taken and the other left. Two women*
> *will be grinding at the mill; one will be taken and the*
> *other left. Watch therefore for you do not know what hour*
> *your Lord is coming. ... Therefore you also be ready for*
> *the Son of Man is coming at an hour you do not expect.'*
> (Matthew 24:38-44)

In other words, people will be carrying on their everyday
lives when suddenly the Lord Jesus will come for those who
believe that He died for our sins and rose again from the
dead. Those who are alive at this time will be taken from the
earth to be with the Lord. This event will happen at a time
when people are carrying on their normal business, doing
normal things like eating and drinking, buying and selling,
planting and building. (See Luke 17:26-37.)

Paul described this event, known as the Rapture of the
Church, in his first letter to the Thessalonians. The word

'Rapture' is taken from the Latin form of the Greek word 'harpazo' used in 1 Thessalonians 4:17 for 'caught up':

*'For the Lord Himself will descend from heaven with a shout, with the voice of an archangel, and with the trumpet of God. And the dead in Christ will rise first. Then we who are alive will be **caught up** to meet the Lord in the air. And thus we shall always be with the Lord. Therefore comfort one another with these words.'*

(1 Thessalonians 4:16-18)

The Bible tells us that the Rapture will come unexpectedly, like a thief in the night, at a time when people are saying 'Peace and Safety':

'But concerning the times and the seasons brethren you have no need that I should write to you. For you yourselves know perfectly that the day of the Lord so comes as a thief in the night. For when they say 'Peace and Safety!' then sudden destruction comes upon them as labour pains on a pregnant woman. And they shall not escape. But you brethren are not in darkness so that this day should overtake you as a thief.'

(1 Thessalonians 5:1-4)

What happens next? In 1 Corinthians 15:51-54 we read:

'Behold, I tell you a mystery: We shall not all sleep, but we shall all be changed— in a moment, in the twinkling of an eye, at the last trumpet. For the trumpet will sound, and the dead will be raised incorruptible, and we shall be changed. For this corruptible must put on incorruption, and this mortal must put on immortality. So when this corruptible has put on incorruption, and this mortal has

put on immortality, then shall be brought to pass the
saying that is written: "Death is swallowed up in victory."'

This means that those who are taken in the Rapture will be given new eternal bodies which will no longer be subject to corruption and mortality. In other words they will never get old or sick or tired and never die. These new bodies will be able to live in the glorious state in which we will always be with the Lord. Those who have already died in Christ will be resurrected and united with those who are alive at the time of the Rapture (1 Thessalonians 4:13-18).

We will appear before the judgement seat of Christ when our lives will be judged according to what we have done (2 Corinthians 5:10). This will be for our rewards, not for heaven or hell. We will be taken to the glorious Marriage Supper of the Lamb (Revelation 19:7-10) then follow Jesus as He returns to the earth as King of kings and Lord of lords to destroy the armies of the Beast (Revelation 19:11-21). We will join with Him in the millennial kingdom in which the Lord will reign over the nations (Isaiah 2:1-4, 11-12, Zechariah 14, Revelation 20). Sounds like an exciting prospect to me! This is the good news about the Second Coming.

The Great Tribulation

The bad news is that this age will end with a time of unique trouble on the earth. Jesus warned that:

'Then there will be great tribulation such as has not been
since the beginning of the world until this time, no, nor
ever shall be. And unless those days were shortened no
flesh would be saved. But for the elect's sake those days
will be shortened.'

(Matthew 24:21-22)

This clearly cannot speak about any time that has already happened (for example the Fall of the Temple in AD 70 or the Nazi Holocaust) because Jesus says it will end with *'the Son of Man coming on the clouds of heaven with power and great glory.'* The implication of those days being shortened is that if they were not *'no flesh would be saved'*, in other words all life would come to an end.

Luke 21:25-28 is a parallel passage to this one describing the Great Tribulation. At this time a massive crisis will hit the world described as the *'distress of nations in perplexity.'* The Greek word used for 'in perplexity' is 'aporia' which literally means 'with no way out'. A global crisis with the powers of the heavens shaken causes *'men's hearts to fail them for fear of what is coming on the world.'* At this time people will be divided between those who reject Jesus and are terrified at the events taking place and those who accept Him and know that their redemption is drawing near (i.e. Jesus is about to come).

The Great Tribulation is prophesied in detail in the Book of Revelation, chapters 6-19. This is a seven-year period which is also described in the Book of Daniel. During this period the Four Horsemen of the Apocalypse ride out bringing false peace, war, famine and death. As a result one quarter of the world's population is killed. Judgements fall on the earth in the form of the seven seals, the seven trumpets and the seven bowls. A further third of the world's population are killed as a result of the destruction that comes on the earth in the seven trumpet judgements. Working on the present number of people in the world, this means about three billion people will be killed in these judgements alone.

Satan gets his man, the Beast or Antichrist, into a position of world power. He has an accomplice, the False Prophet, who sets up the mark of the Beast system in which people are given a number and a mark without which they cannot buy or sell. Finally, the nations of the world gather together for the last battle, Armageddon. Then the Lord Jesus will return in power and glory to defeat the armies of the Beast and the False Prophet, bind Satan and throw him into the abyss and reign on the earth during the 1000 period known as the Millennium (Revelation 19-20). This is the same event as the time prophesied in Isaiah 2:1-4, when the Messiah reigns from Jerusalem when the earth will be restored to peace and harmony.

Which comes first – the Rapture or the Tribulation?

This raises an issue which often divides Christians. Is the Rapture of the Church a separate event from the second coming of Christ to the earth, or is it all part of the same event? Does it come before, in the middle of, or at the end of, the Great Tribulation?

The belief that the Rapture comes before the Great Tribulation is based on the fact that there are several significant differences in Bible passages dealing with the Rapture and those which deal with the second coming to the earth. The table opposite compares some of these differences.

The most obvious difference is that at the Rapture believers will be caught up in the clouds to meet the Lord in the air, while at His Glorious Appearing Jesus returns to earth with the saints. In other words, at the Rapture, Jesus receives the saints (i.e. true believers in the Lord Jesus) to Himself.

As we have already seen, this event will be unexpected, like a 'thief in the night.' The only way the Rapture can be unexpected is if it comes before the Great Tribulation. By the end of this time it will be obvious that Jesus is coming back to the earth as the armies gather at Armageddon 3½ years after the Antichrist and the False Prophet set up the Mark of

Rapture	Second coming to the earth
Christ comes for His own. (John 14:3; 1 Thessalonians 4:17)	Christ comes with His own. (Jude 14-15; Revelation 1:7; 19:14)
He comes in the air. (1 Thessalonians 4:17)	He comes to the earth. (Zechariah 14:4-5; Acts 1:11)
He comes to claim His bride. (The true Church) (John 14:3; 1 Thessalonians 4:16-17)	He returns with His bride. (Revelation 19:6-14)
Only His own see Him (1 Thessalonians 4:13-18)	Every eye shall see Him. (Revelation 1:7; Matthew 24:30)
Saved are delivered from wrath. (1 Thessalonians 1:10; 5:9)	Unsaved experience the wrath of God. (Isaiah 2.10-21; Revelation 6.12-17)

the Beast system. No one will be saying "Peace and Safety" after the horrors of the Great Tribulation. Life will not be going on as normal. And you should even be able to work out the date – 42 months after the setting up of the image to the Beast in Revelation 13.

Should we tell people to be ready for the Rapture or for trouble?

Since we do not know the day or the hour of the coming of the Lord, or the hour of our death, we should be ready to meet the Lord all the time. We do this by repenting of sin and believing that Jesus died for our sins and rose again from the dead. When we do this we are 'born again' of the

Holy Spirit. The work of the Holy Spirit in our lives is in order to purify us from sin and change us from the person we were before we came to know the Lord.

John wrote about the coming of the Lord:

'We know that when He is revealed, we shall be like Him, for we shall see Him as He is. And everyone who has this hope in Him purifies himself, just as He is pure.'

(1 John 3:2-3)

If we believe that Jesus could come for us at any time, it means that we want to be found by Him doing what is pleasing to Him, not what is wicked in His sight. So, yes, we should be ready for the Rapture to come or to be taken by the Lord at our death.

At the same time we know that many people are going through intense times of trouble now, victims of poverty, wars and natural disasters, which affect Christians along with the rest of the population. In much of the world Christians face persecution for their faith. As we get nearer the time of the Great Tribulation we can expect the troubles of the world to intensify. These troubles may affect those in the West who have led comparatively easy lives and not suffered the persecutions of Christians in places like China or the Muslim world, or the poverty of Christians in parts of Africa, Asia and South America. So we should also be ready for trouble to come as we approach the end of the age.

What is clear is that the time of the Great Tribulation will come out of a world already in the grip of great wickedness which is rejecting God's Word and salvation through Jesus the Messiah. Already we have seen great persecutions of Christians in the Communist world during the 20th century, the horrors of the Nazi Holocaust in Europe, continuing suffering of people in many countries of the world as a result of evil governments, wars, famines and natural disasters. As we shall see in this book, many forces of evil are being unleashed in our time which will reach their climax in the Great Tribulation period.

On this basis, I believe that a study of prophecy should also prepare Christians for the likelihood of a time of trouble coming on the earth. The 'distress of nations' of which Jesus spoke in Luke 21 as a sign of His second coming is almost upon us. On present trends I would expect most countries of the world (including Britain and America) to be in the hands of anti-Christian powers in the not too distant future. These powers are likely to suppress the true message of the Gospel and persecute genuine Christians. So if the Rapture is delayed by this amount of time we need to be ready for a time of trouble.

In the end only the Lord can decide the date of His return. God will overrule so that His purposes will stand despite the fact that most of the world is in rebellion against Him. While time remains God wants us to tell people that Jesus is the Messiah and Saviour who has come once to save us from our sins, and who is coming again to judge the world in righteousness.

SIGNS IN ISRAEL

4 *Biblical Prophecies About Israel*

IIIIIIIIIIIIIIIIIIIIIIIIIIIIIIIIIIIIIIIIIIIIIIIIIIIIIIIIIIIIIIIIIIIIIIIIIIIIIIIIIIIIIIIIIIIIIIIIIIIIIIIIIIIIIIIIIIIIIIIIIIIIIII

The Bible contains a number of prophecies relating to Israel in the last days of this age (in the Old Testament the time before the *'Day of the Lord'* and in the New Testament the time before the Second Coming of Christ). Many of these speak of the following happening:

◊ A return of the Jewish people to the land of Israel.
◊ A time of trouble.
◊ An outpouring of the Holy Spirit.

Christians in Britain don't hear much about this because most of the Church today either ignores this subject altogether or believes in 'replacement theology' – that the prophecies about the return of the Jewish people to Israel only apply to the Church. So, for example, where the Lord says about gathering the *'outcasts of Israel'* from the north, south, east and west (Isaiah 11:12, 43:5-6), replacement theology teaches that Jesus means the gathering of people into the kingdom of God (i.e. the Church):

> *'They will come from the east and the west, from the north and the south, and sit in the kingdom of God.'*
> (Luke 13:29)

According to this view, when God made the new covenant through Jesus the Messiah, He annulled the former covenants made with Abraham concerning the people and the land of Israel and through Moses concerning the Law (Torah).

On the other hand those who take a literal historical view of Scripture believe that God's covenant with Israel remains in place and so what happens in relation to Israel is significant. That is the view I am taking in this book.

In Jeremiah 31:10 we read:

> *'Hear the word of the LORD, O nations, and declare it in the isles afar off, and say, "He who scattered Israel will gather him, and keep him as a shepherd does his flock."'*

Here the Lord promises that Israel will be kept as a people even after they are scattered among the nations and from there they will be gathered again to the land of Israel.

This is a word which the Lord wants the nations (the Hebrew word is 'goyim' or Gentiles) to hear and for this to be declared in the 'isles afar off'. In Hebrew prophecy the 'isles afar off' represent the nations out of the region of the Middle Eastern countries – like Britain, America, Australia and distant parts of Africa and Asia. In the time of Jeremiah and the deportation of the Jews to Babylon there would have been no point in declaring this word to these countries because they would have had no knowledge of events relating to Israel and not much interest either! Today people all over the world know where Israel is and events taking place there are frequently in the news. So there is a point in 'declaring' this message even in lands on the other side of the world from Israel today. Those who accept the Hebrew prophets as part of the Bible (i.e. Christians) should 'hear' (pay attention to and note) what is happening with the Jewish people. They have literally been scattered into the nations of the world and now in our time they have been regathered to Israel.

The Lord Jesus spoke about the dispersion of the Jewish people from Jerusalem following the destruction of the Temple and of Jerusalem in Luke 21:20-24:

> 'But when you see Jerusalem surrounded by armies, then know that its desolation is near. Then let those who are in Judea flee to the mountains, let those who are in the midst of her depart, and let not those who are in the country enter her. For these are the days of vengeance, that all things which are written may be fulfilled. But woe to those who are pregnant and to those who are nursing babies in those days! For there will be great distress in the land and wrath upon this people. And they will fall by the edge of the sword, and be led away captive into all nations. And Jerusalem will be trampled by Gentiles until the times of the Gentiles are fulfilled.'

From this we see that the dispersion of the Jews will not be a permanent condition. The day will come when Jerusalem will no longer be 'trampled' or ruled by the Gentiles and 'the fig tree' of Israel's national life will blossom again:

> 'Then He spoke to them a parable: "Look at the fig tree, and all the trees. When they are already budding, you see and know for yourselves that summer is now near. So you also, when you see these things happening, know that the kingdom of God is near. Assuredly, I say to you, this generation will by no means pass away till all things take place. Heaven and earth will pass away, but My words will by no means pass away."'

(Luke 21:29-33)

The fig tree is used as a symbol of Israel's national life in Hosea 9:10 and Jeremiah 24. When Jesus spoke of the fig tree that would be 'cut down' if it did not bear fruit in Luke 13:6-9, He was clearly speaking about Israel not bearing the fruit of God's righteousness and the coming judgement on Israel with the fall of Jerusalem and the dispersion of the Jewish people. When Jesus cursed the fig tree and caused it to wither in Matthew 21:19 this unusual miracle (actually the only 'negative' miracle which Jesus did – all His other miracles were beneficial) had a spiritual meaning – that the national life of Israel was about to wither.

The budding of the fig tree was to be a visual aid to people around the world of a greater event which is to follow – the return of the Messiah. Jesus makes this clear in Matthew 24:32-33:

'Now learn this parable from the fig tree: When its
branch has already become tender and puts forth leaves,
you know that summer is near. So you also, when you see
all these things, know that it is near—at the doors!'

The budding of the fig tree – the rebirth of Israel as a nation along with all the other signs of the second coming which are taking place in our time – is a wake up call to the world that Jesus is coming back.

The Covenant with Abraham

Nearly 4000 years ago God made a covenant with Abraham, making him two amazing promises:

'Look now toward heaven and count the stars if you are
able to number them. So shall your descendants be.'

(Genesis 15:5)

> *'I am the Lord, who brought you out of Ur of the*
> *Chaldeans to give you this land to inherit it.'*
>
> (Genesis 15:7)

Here we find the promises that God made to Abraham. Firstly he will have innumerable descendants, a promise which Abraham believed. So the Lord *'accounted it to him for righteousness'* (i.e. He confirmed the promise on the basis of Abraham's faith). Today a vast number of people claim descent in some form from Abraham. Secondly God promised that Abraham's descendants would inherit the land of Canaan / Israel. Concerning this promise God did something which we find hard to understand, but Abraham would have had no problem understanding. He told Abraham to take some animals, *'a three year old heifer, a three year old female goat, a three year old ram, a turtledove and a young pigeon'* (Genesis 15:9) and to cut them in two and leave a path between the pieces of the divided animals. Then *'there appeared a smoking oven and a burning torch that passed between those pieces'* (Genesis 15:17). The smoking oven and burning torch represent the presence of God, which passed between the divided animals.

> *'On the same day the Lord made a covenant with*
> *Abram saying, "To your descendants I have given this*
> *land, from the river of Egypt to the great river, the*
> *River Euphrates."'*
>
> (Genesis 15:18)

What was all this about? In Abraham's culture if two parties were making a land deal, they did not go to the estate agent and the solicitor. They cut animals in two, passed between the divided animals and said in effect, 'May God (or the gods) do to us as we have done to these animals if we do not keep our word.' Now it was not the best day in the life of those animals when they were cut in two, so the people making the covenant were invoking a curse upon themselves if they did not keep their word. God put Abraham to sleep so that he did not have to pass between the divided animals. By doing this God was communicating something very important. This covenant, by which He was giving the title deeds of ownership of the land to Abraham and his descendants, depended on God's faithfulness, not theirs. God would keep His side of the covenant despite the unfaithfulness of Abraham's descendants.

The major problem from Abraham's point of view was that he did not have even one descendant, let alone a multitude, and his wife Sarah was barren and past childbearing age. So Sarah suggested that Abraham had a child by Hagar, her maid, which he did. So Ishmael was born – but God told Abraham that this son would not inherit the promise. Instead, Sarah would have a son supernaturally and this child was to be called Isaac:

> *'Sarah your wife shall bear you a son, and you shall call his name Isaac; I will establish my covenant with him for an everlasting covenant and with his descendants after him. As for Ishmael, I have heard you. Behold I have blessed him, and will make him fruitful and will multiply him exceedingly. He shall beget twelve princes and I will make him a great nation.'*
>
> (Genesis 17:19-20)

God says that the covenant relating to the land applies to Isaac and his descendants and not to Ishmael and his descendants. Ishmael will become a great nation, but the covenant will be with Isaac. Today the conflict over the land of Israel involves the Jewish people, who claim descent from Isaac, and the

Arab people, who claim descent from Ishmael. In Islam, the dominant religion of the Arabs, Abraham is believed to be a prophet of Islam and the promised son is believed to be Ishmael and not Isaac. Therefore the promises given to Abraham are attributed to Ishmael and his descendants, the Arabs, and not to the Jews.

However in the Bible it is clear that the promise is given to the descendants of Abraham, Isaac and Jacob (i.e. the children of Israel). The promise given to Abraham was repeated to Isaac (Genesis 26:2-5) and to Jacob (Genesis 28:13-15). It was the basis on which God called Moses to lead the Israelites out of Egypt into the Promised Land (Exodus 6:6-8). As they made their way through the wilderness God gave them the Torah (Law / commandments), which He told them to live by. God also made provision for their failure to keep His commandments, by giving them a system of sacrifices to be offered at the Tabernacle and later at the Temple, by means of which they could receive atonement and forgiveness for their sins.

According to Deuteronomy 28, if they obeyed the Lord they would enjoy the land with good harvests, peace and prosperity, and they would defeat their enemies and be a light to the surrounding nations. But if they worshipped other gods and disobeyed God's commandments, a series of disasters would come upon them as a judgement, with the final judgement being removal from the land:

'You will be left few in number, whereas you were as the stars of heaven in multitude, because you would not obey the voice of the Lord your God. And it shall be that just as the Lord rejoiced over you to do you good and multiply you, so the Lord will rejoice over you to destroy you and bring you to nothing; and you shall be plucked off the land, which you go to possess. Then the Lord will

scatter you among all peoples from one end of the earth
to the other.'

(Deuteronomy 28:62-64)

In these verses we see the reversal of the promise given
to Abraham. They would become few in number and be
removed from the land. However, even if this most severe
judgement took place, they would not be permanently out of
the land but would return in God's time:

'If any of you are driven out to the farthest parts under
heaven, from there the Lord your God will gather you
and from there He will bring you. Then the Lord your
God will bring you to the land which your fathers
possessed, and you shall possess it.'

(Deuteronomy 30:4-5)

Much of the Old Testament can be seen as the outworking of
these principles. At times when Israel was faithful to the Lord
they were blessed in the land and overcame their enemies.
At the height of Israelite power under David and Solomon
they reached for a brief while the promised boundaries
of the land (2 Samuel 8:3, 1 Kings 4:21). But more often
disobedience to the Lord and the worship of other gods
caused Israel to be diminished by the surrounding nations,
and eventually to suffer exile from the land (2 Kings 17: 24-5,
2 Chronicles 36:14-21).

Jeremiah was the prophet who God raised up to speak to
the generation before the deportation of the Jewish people to
Babylon. As a prophet he did three main things:

◊ He told them what was going to happen.

◊ He gave a reason for it.

◊ He gave a promise of restoration.

For forty years Jeremiah warned his generation that the Babylonians were going to invade and destroy Jerusalem and the Temple and take them into captivity unless they repented of their sins. The reason why it was going to happen was the worship of idols and the breaking of God's commandments:

> *'Behold you trust in lying words that cannot profit. Will you steal, murder, commit adultery, swear falsely, burn incense to Baal, and walk after other gods whom you do not know, and then come and stand before Me in this house which is called by My name and say, "We are delivered to do all these abominations?"'*
>
> (Jeremiah 7:8-10)

Far from repenting, Jeremiah was mocked and rejected as the people preferred false prophets who said they were going to have peace and safety. But Jeremiah was not just a prophet of doom. He also promised a return from Babylon:

> *'For thus says the Lord: "After seventy years are completed at Babylon, I will visit you and perform my good word toward you, and cause you to return to this place. For I know the thoughts that I have towards you says the Lord, thoughts of peace and not of evil, to give you a future and a hope."'*
>
> (Jeremiah 29:10-11)

This promise was fulfilled when the Persians overthrew the Babylonian Empire and the Persian Emperor Cyrus issued a decree that the Jewish people should return to the Promised Land and rebuild the Temple in Jerusalem (Ezra 1:1-4). In this way the covenant was being fulfilled as the descendants of Abraham returned to the land God promised to Abraham.

Jeremiah looked further ahead than the return of the Jews from Babylon. He prophesied a time when God would make a new covenant with the house of Israel through which their sins would be forgiven:

'Behold, the days are coming, says the Lord, when I will make a new covenant with the house of Israel and with the house of Judah—not according to the covenant that I made with their fathers in the day that I took them by the hand to lead them out of the land of Egypt, My covenant which they broke, though I was a husband to them, says the Lord. But this is the covenant that I will make with the house of Israel after those days, says the Lord: I will put My law in their minds, and write it on their hearts; and I will be their God, and they shall be My people. No more shall every man teach his neighbour, and every man his brother, saying, "Know the Lord," for they all shall know Me, from the least of them to the greatest of them, says the Lord. For I will forgive their iniquity, and their sin I will remember no more.'

(Jeremiah 31:31-34)

Here God refers to the covenant made through Moses at Sinai after the Exodus as a 'broken' covenant which Israel was not able to keep. He promises a new covenant through which sin will be forgiven and God's law will be written on the heart of His people and they will know the Lord. All of these provisions are made through the sacrifice of Yeshua (Jesus) and the new covenant which He has brought in. Whether or not professing Christians are faithful to this covenant does not affect its validity from God's point of view. Those of us who call on the Lord in repentance and faith in the Messiah Jesus who died for our sins and rose again from the dead know that our sins are forgiven. God also writes His law on our hearts through the Holy Spirit being given to us and we come to know the Lord as our Saviour.

On the other hand God has not removed the covenant He made with Abraham. Significantly the very next verses, in Jeremiah 31:35-36, read:

'Thus says the Lord, Who gives the sun for a light by day, the ordinances of the moon and the stars for a light by night, Who disturbs the sea, and its waves roar (The Lord of hosts is His name): "If those ordinances depart from before Me, says the Lord, then the seed of Israel shall also cease from being a nation before Me forever."'

In other words after the giving of the new covenant, Israel will remain a nation before the Lord, even in the dispersion.

The new covenant points to the Messiah who was to come to deal with the problem of sin, which causes us all to break God's commandments. According to Isaiah 53, this One would be the Suffering Servant of the Lord:

'He is despised and rejected of men, a man of sorrows and acquainted with grief. And we hid, as it were our faces from Him; He was despised and we did not esteem Him. Surely He has born our griefs and carried our sorrows; Yet we esteemed Him stricken, smitten by God and afflicted. But He was wounded for our transgressions, He was bruised for our iniquities; the chastisement of our peace was upon Him, and by His stripes we are healed. All we like sheep have gone astray; we have turned every one to his own way and the Lord has laid on Him the iniquity of us all.'

(Isaiah 53:3-6)

When Jesus came in fulfilment of this and many other prophecies, He brought in the New Covenant, through dying as a sacrifice for the sins of the world at the time of the Passover. At the time that the Jewish people were offering the Passover lambs to remember the blood of the lamb, which protected them from the Angel of Death (see Exodus 12), Jesus was put to death by crucifixion in fulfilment of Psalm 22, Daniel 9:26 and Zechariah 12:10. He was the *'Lamb of God who takes away the sin of the world'* (John 1:29). He saves all those who come under the protection of His blood from eternal death.

Did the coming of the New Covenant mean that God was finished with the Jewish people and that the covenant made with Abraham no longer applied? Much of the Church actually teaches this. But as we have seen, after God gave His promise of the new covenant He said that as long as the sun, the moon and the stars exist, so long will Israel be a nation before the Lord (Jeremiah 31:35-36).

If we look carefully at Jesus' words we discover that in relation to Israel, Jesus too functioned in the same prophetic way that Jeremiah did:

◊ He warned of the coming catastrophe.

◊ He gave a reason for it.

◊ He gave a promise of restoration.

As Jesus was riding into Jerusalem at the beginning of the week which would lead up to his crucifixion and resurrection, He stopped half way down the Mount of Olives and wept over the city. He said:

'If you had known, even you, especially in this your day, the things that make for your peace! But now they are hidden from your eyes. For the days will come upon you

when your enemies will build an embankment around
you, surround you and level you and your children within
you to the ground; and they will not leave on you one
stone upon another, because you did not know the time of
your visitation.'

(Luke 19:41-44)

Jesus prophesied the coming destruction of Jerusalem and the Temple by the Romans in 70AD. He told those who believed in Him to flee from the city when they saw the armies gathering, because this was going to lead to a time of terrible slaughter and destruction:

'For there will be great distress in the land and wrath
upon this people. And they shall fall by the edge of the
sword and be led away captive into all nations. And
Jerusalem will be trampled by Gentiles until the times of
the Gentiles are fulfilled.'

(Luke 21:20-24)

In these verses Jesus warned of the coming destruction of Jerusalem, and the dispersion of the Jewish people into the lands of the Gentiles. He also gave a reason for it: "Because you did not know the time of your visitation". In other words, the dispersion happened because of the failure to recognise Jesus as the Messiah and to believe that He died as a sacrifice for the sins of the world and rose again from the dead, as the Apostles taught. Of course the twelve disciples were all Jewish and there were many Jewish people who did recognise Jesus as Messiah. Through them the faith went out into all the world. But the Jewish religious leadership rejected His claim and continued to offer the animal sacrifices for sin in the Temple, after Jesus had come as the final sacrifice for sin. After the sacrifice of Jesus, the offering of the sacrifices became an act of unbelief, rather than faith, because the blood of the animals had been replaced with the blood of Jesus as the means whereby sin was atoned for. The Letter to the Hebrews warns Jewish believers in Jesus not to go back to the animal sacrifices in the Temple.

For this reason Jesus said:

> *'Your house (the Temple) is left to you desolate; for I say to you (i.e. Jerusalem), you shall see me no more until you say "Blessed is He who comes in the name of the Lord."'*
>
> (Matthew 23:38-9)

'Blessed is he who comes in the name of the Lord' is not just any old phrase. In Hebrew it is 'Baruch ha ba be shem Adonai', the traditional greeting for the coming Messiah.

In this verse, Jesus was not only pointing to the desolation in Jerusalem which happened with the destruction of the Temple in 70AD, but also to the time when the desolation of Jerusalem will be reversed. The revelation of Jesus as the Messiah will cause this change in the fortunes of the city as the Jewish people will call out to Him to return. Then He will come as the Reigning King Messiah and Jerusalem will no longer be *'trampled* (ruled*) by the Gentiles'* (Luke 21:24).

A number of Old Testament prophecies tie in with this. In Ezekiel 36-37 there are prophecies of a physical restoration of Israel, from being a barren land, denuded of its trees and with its cities forsaken, to becoming a fertile land 'like the Garden of Eden.' There is also a prophecy of the spiritual restoration of the people:

> *'For I will take you from among the nations, gather you out of all countries and bring you into your own land. Then I will sprinkle clean water on you and you shall be*

*clean; I will cleanse you from all your filthiness and from
all your idols. I will give you a new heart and put a new
spirit within you; I will take the heart of stone out of your
flesh and give you a heart of flesh. I will put my Spirit
within you and cause you to walk in My statutes, and you
will keep My judgements and do them. Then you shall
dwell in the land that I gave to your fathers; you shall be
My people and I will be your God.'*

(Ezekiel 36:24-28)

Ezekiel 37 speaks of the '*dry bones*' of Israel coming to life
and then the Spirit blowing on them and causing them to
arise. This passage points to Israel being born of the flesh
and then born of the spirit, the very process which Jesus
spoke to Nicodemus about when he said:

*'That which is born of the flesh is flesh and that which is
born of the spirit is spirit. Do not marvel that I said unto
you, "You must be born again."'*

(John 3:6-7)

The Covenant with Moses

The main event of the Torah (the first five books of the
Bible) to which all of the rest of the Old Testament looks
back is the Exodus from Egypt and the giving of the Law /
Torah at Mount Sinai. God gave Israel the Commandments
through Moses at Sinai (Exodus 20). In Leviticus 26 and
Deuteronomy 28 God shows Israel that if they are faithful to
the Lord and keep His commandments He will bless them in
the land. He will deliver them from their enemies, give them
good harvests and make them a witness to the nations round
about of what it is to have the Lord as their God. But if they
are unfaithful and go after other gods of the nations round

about them and break God's commandments, then He will bring a series of judgements upon them. The last and most severe of these judgements is to be cast out of the land and dwell amongst the Gentiles. But God also promises that He will bring them back again on the basis of the covenant with Abraham which we have looked at before.

The New Testament shows that God has replaced the covenant with Moses as the way in which we approach God. Jesus' sacrifice for sin on the cross replaces the animal sacrifices prescribed in Leviticus and Jesus Himself becomes our High Priest who mediates salvation. Therefore the Levitical priesthood and the animal sacrifices are no longer required to do away with sin. Significantly God gave Israel 40 years to learn this lesson after which the Temple was destroyed and the sacrifices and the Levitical priesthood ceased.

When the Temple was destroyed in 70AD by the Romans, the Sanhedrin reconvened in Yavneh (Jamnia) under the leadership of Rabbi Yochanan ben Zakkai, who developed a theology which became the basis of Judaism today. The Temple no longer stood and therefore there was no access to the place appointed by God to offer the sacrifices. As a result of this teaching it was believed that God was able to forgive sins through repentance, prayers, fasting and good deeds which replaced the blood of the animal sacrifices.

This led to the development of Talmudic Judaism. According to this view, when Moses received the written Torah recorded in the first five books of the Bible, he also received an unwritten set of instructions known as the Oral Law, showing how to apply the written law. This was said to have been passed on by word of mouth from generation to generation until around 200AD when Rabbi Judah Hanasi compiled the document called the Mishna.

He saw that the conditions for the Jews were going from bad to worse, with the Temple destroyed, the Sanhedrin no longer able to meet and no central authority functioning as Jews fled the land of Israel and endured persecutions. In order to preserve the oral traditions he decided the time had come to write them down, so he went to as many rabbis as he could in order to extract from them their entire memories. He put those recollections together, edited them and the result was the Mishna (which means repetition). A commentary on the Mishna was added called the Gemara, the entire compilation being known as the Talmud. This form of Judaism explained the absence of the sacrifices and said that God was pleased to accept prayer, fasting and good deeds to cover sin, thus replacing the animal sacrifices required on the Day of Atonement (Yom Kippur) in Leviticus 16-17.

This was actually a fulfilment of the prophecy of Hosea concerning Israel:

> *'For the children of Israel shall abide many days without king or prince, without sacrifice or sacred pillar, without ephod or teraphim. Afterward the children of Israel shall return and seek the LORD their God and David their king. They shall fear the LORD and His goodness in the latter days.'*

(Hosea 3:4-5)

'Many days' here means a long period of time during which there will be no central authority for the Jewish people (king or prince), no sacrifice for sin and no revelation from God. As a result of this the prophetic word became as a *'sealed book'* in which the religion was based more on man made rules than the word of God as was prophesied in Isaiah 29:10-13. However, it is clear from the Scriptures that this is not to be the permanent condition of Israel. In the prophecy above,

Hosea wrote that after *'many days'* during which there was no king, sacrifice or revelation, Israel would seek the Lord.

The Problem of Christianity

In the first century many Jews believed that Jesus was the Messiah who shed His blood as an atonement for sin. Those who understood this realised that the blood of Jesus had replaced the blood of the animal sacrifices offered by the High Priest in the Temple as the letter to the Hebrews explains:

> *'According to the law almost all things are purified*
> *with blood, and without shedding of blood there is no*
> *remission. ... Now, once at the end of the ages, He*
> *(Messiah) has appeared to put away sin by the sacrifice*
> *of Himself. And as it is appointed for men to die once,*
> *but after this the judgment, so Messiah was offered once*
> *to bear the sins of many. To those who eagerly wait*
> *for Him He will appear a second time, apart from sin,*
> *for salvation.'*
>
> (Hebrews 9:22-28)

At the same time the majority of Jewish people rejected Jesus as Saviour in the early years of the Messianic faith. But this did not mean that Christians should reject the Jewish people. In his letter to the Romans (chapters 9 to 11) Paul told the Gentile Christians to pray for Israel's salvation and to remember the Jewish roots of the faith. He looked forward to the day when Israel would be saved and reminded the Romans that the Jewish people are *'beloved for the sake of the fathers.'* (Romans 11:28).

However the Romans and the majority of Christians ignored Paul's message. As more and more Gentiles entered the Church, an anti-Jewish spirit took over, which ended up condemning the Jewish people as Christ killers and breaking all links with the Jewish roots of Christianity. At the Council of Nicea in 325AD the Roman Emperor Constantine said, "It is right to demand what our reason approves and that we should have nothing in common with the Jews."

This resulted in the development of the Roman Catholic and Eastern Orthodox Churches and the imposition of a form of Christianity which Jesus and the Apostles would hardly have recognised. Instead of offering salvation and life to all, it became an oppressive religious political system which denied the fact that Jesus died as the Saviour of all humanity, Jewish and Gentile, and that He came firstly for the Jewish people. It placed the entire Jewish people under a curse as 'Christ killers.'

This goes against the teaching of the New Testament. Jesus said of His approaching death:

'Therefore My Father loves Me, because I lay down My life that I may take it again. No one takes it from Me, but I lay it down of Myself. I have power to lay it down, and I have power to take it again. This command I have received from My Father.'

(John 10:17-18)

Here Jesus says that He was voluntarily laying down His life as a sacrifice for the sin of the world. Through His death God's purpose would be fulfilled.

On the human side there was a Jewish and a Gentile responsibility, as is made clear in the Book of Acts:

'For truly against Your holy Servant Jesus, whom You anointed, both Herod and Pontius Pilate, with the Gentiles and the people of Israel, were gathered together to do whatever Your hand and Your purpose determined before to be done.'

(Acts 4:27-28)

This passage shows that the ultimate responsibility for the death of Jesus is with God Himself in order that God's predetermined purpose would be fulfilled. This is also made clear in the prophecy of Isaiah 53:10:

> 'Yet it pleased the LORD to bruise Him; He has put Him to grief, when You make His soul an offering for sin.'

In a sense, we all killed Jesus because we are all sinners and He died for our sins. But His death is in order that our sins may be forgiven through the Gospel (good news). This good news is for both Jews and Gentiles:

> 'For I am not ashamed of the gospel of Messiah, for it is the power of God to salvation for everyone who believes, for the Jew first and also for the Greek. For in it the righteousness of God is revealed from faith to faith; as it is written, "The just shall live by faith."'
>
> (Romans 1:16-17)

As the Church rejected its Jewish roots and the Jewish people – exactly what Paul said it should not do in Romans 9-11 – so Jewish people began to see 'Christianity' as a hostile anti-Semitic religion.

A Time of Trouble

Paul encouraged the early Christians to pray for the salvation of Israel (Romans 10) which is what God wants us to do today. He also showed that there is a day coming when salvation will come to Israel:

> 'Blindness in part has happened to Israel, until the fullness of the Gentiles come in. And so all Israel shall be

*saved; as it is written: "There shall come out of Zion the
Deliverer, and shall turn away ungodliness from Jacob;
for this is my covenant unto them, when I shall take away
their sins". As concerning the gospel they are enemies
for your sakes; but as touching the election, they are
beloved for the fathers' sakes. For the gifts and calling of
God are without repentance.'*

(Romans 11:25-29)

End time scriptures show that God wants to bring Jewish
people to recognise Jesus as the Messiah. He will bring this
to pass through 'the time of Jacob's trouble':

*'For thus says the Lord: "We have heard a voice of
trembling, of fear, and not of peace. Ask now and see
whether a man is ever in labour with child? So why do I
see every man with his hands on his loins like a woman
in labour and all faces turned pale? Alas! For that day is
great, so that none is like it; and it is the time of Jacob's
trouble, but he shall be saved out of it."'*

(Jeremiah 30:4-7)

(See also Ezekiel 38-9, Daniel 12, Joel 2-3, Zechariah 12-14,
Matthew 24, Luke 21 and Revelation 6-19).

This time of trouble is equivalent to the Great Tribulation.
It involves all nations and precedes the event known in
the Old Testament as the *Day of the Lord* and in the New
Testament as the Second Coming of Jesus Christ. In this
time of trouble God is seeking to correct something, which
Israel has got wrong:

*"For I am with you," says the Lord, "to save you;
though I make a full end of all nations where I have
scattered you, yet will I not make a complete end of you.*

*But I will correct you in justice and not let you altogether
go unpunished."*

(Jeremiah 30:11)

What could this be? Israeli treatment of the Palestinians? The
fact that Israel is a secular state? All the different branches
of Judaism and the often hostile relations between them? Or
the identity of the Messiah?

If you were to ask 100 Jewish people how they would
identify the Messiah, you would come up with maybe not
100, but certainly a good number of different answers. These
are some of the main ones I have heard:

◊ Messiah is a great man who will create world peace,
rebuild the Temple in Jerusalem and bring the Jewish
people back to the Torah.

◊ Messiah is Rabbi Schneerson of Lubavitch, who died in
1994 and who will rise again from the dead.

◊ There is no personal Messiah, but there will be a
Messianic age in which people will live in peace and
harmony together and wars will cease.

◊ There is no Messiah and the whole idea is a superstition,
which Jewish people need to put behind them so they can
work out their problems by themselves.

◊ Yeshua / Jesus is the Messiah who has come once and is
coming again.

God's will is that Israel should come to believe the last
option on this list.

Israel and the Messiah

At the beginning of the twentieth century, there was some
hostility between Orthodox Judaism and Zionism. The goal
of secular Zionism was to become 'a nation like all others.'

This meant that Jewish identity was to be found in a national identity rather than a religious one. Because of this, many rabbis condemned secular Zionism as an attempt to destroy the Torah and traditional Judaism. They taught that first the Messiah has to come and then he will cause the Jews to return to Israel, rebuild the Temple and create world peace.

The novel by Chaim Potok, *The Chosen*, set in New York just after the Second World War, gives a good insight into this conflict within Jewish thinking. It features the friendship between Reuven Malter, the son of a Zionist activist campaigning for the Jewish state in Palestine, and Danny, the son of Reb Saunders, a Hassidic rabbi who vehemently opposes the establishment of a Jewish state before the arrival of the Messiah. When Reuven's father makes a speech at a pro-Israel rally that is printed in the newspapers, Reb Saunders forbids Danny to speak to Reuven, or even mention his name. Their friendship resumes after the State of Israel is founded in May 1948; Danny explains to Reuven that Reb Saunders has relented, since the new nation is 'no longer an issue; it's a fact.'

The main influence leading to an acceptance of Zionism by most of mainstream Judaism was Rav (Rabbi) Kook (1865-1935), the Ashkenazi Chief Rabbi of Palestine during the British Mandate period. He heard the 'footsteps of the Messiah' in the modern movement to re-establish a Jewish state in the land of Israel. He believed that even the secular Zionist pioneers could be part of a grand Divine process whereby the land and people of Israel were finally being redeemed from the 2,000-year exile. As Jews sacrificed themselves for the cause of building up the physical land, they were laying the groundwork for the ultimate spiritual messianic redemption of world Jewry. He once commented that the establishment of the Chief Rabbinate was the first step towards the re-establishment of the Sanhedrin. Today many Orthodox Jews see modern Israel as 'the gift God has given us' as the Jewish state has absorbed Jewish people from around the world and become the main centre of Jewish learning.

At the same time we have to acknowledge that 70% of Israelis today are secular and that the same sins which affect western nations are to be found in modern Israel. I once got involved in an internet discussion with an Orthodox Jew who was very critical of what he described as the 'filth' of modern Israel which he typified by gay bars and mixed beaches. He called for people to accept 'the yoke of Torah' which would change the whole moral standing of the country. He said that if Israel and Jewish people worldwide did this then they would deserve the Messiah and he would come by the way of peace. If not there would be a time of calamity leading to the Messiah.

However establishing modern Israel on Torah values is not so easy. When the Jews returned from the first exile after a relatively short period in Babylon, they were a unified people who did return to Torah values as we see in the Books of Ezra and Nehemiah. The Temple was rebuilt and the sacrificial system re-instated. Ezra read from the *'Book of the Law of Moses'* and explained it to the people and instructed teachers who were able to *'give the sense and cause people to understand the reading'* (Nehemiah 8:1-8).

The second restoration of Israel in our time has come after the Jewish people have been dispersed around the world over a very long period of time. During this time they have been exposed to persecution and discrimination both in Christendom and in the Muslim world. They suffered the Holocaust at the hands of the Nazis and an anti-God society under Communism in the Soviet Union. Responses to these experiences from within the Jewish community vary from ultra Orthodoxy to secular humanism.

As a result there is a gulf between those who would like Israel to be a modern secular country and those who wish Israel to be a Torah observant country. Many Israelis are disillusioned with religion and have no belief in the coming of the Messiah. Much of Israel does give the impression of being a country like any other absorbing influences from the rest of the world.

I remember standing in Tel Aviv bus station with McDonalds on one side, a bookstall with semi-pornographic magazines on the other side and rock music blaring out from another stall, and thinking, 'This is a country like any other.' 'Lonely Planet' travel guide has voted Tel Aviv the third 'hottest' city in the world, describing it as 'a modern Sin City on the sea' where there are more 'more bars than synagogues, God is a DJ and everyone's body is a temple. Tel Aviv is also home to a large gay community, a kind of San Francisco in the Middle East.' The Israeli version of 'Strictly Come Dancing' featured a lesbian celebrity, Gili Shem Tov, partnered with another woman. Gili said: "I live with a woman, we are raising my son together and it felt natural to dance with a woman." She hoped her move would make the country more tolerant towards homosexuals.

But then there are other things which show that Israel is not a country like any other. These tie up with the prophecies of the Bible – the restoration of the land with trees planted on the hills and the deserts blooming, the ancient cities being repopulated with Jewish people coming from the four corners of the earth and Israel's deliverance in wars with nations seeking her destruction. Isaiah, Jeremiah, Ezekiel and other prophets foretold this happening.

Ezekiel wrote:

'For I will take you out from among the nations, gather you out of all countries, and bring you into your own

land. Then I will sprinkle clean water on you, and you
shall be clean; I will cleanse you from all your filthiness
and from all your idols. I will give you a new heart and
put a new spirit within you; I will take out the heart of
stone out of your flesh and give you a heart of flesh. I
will put my Spirit within you and cause you to walk in
My statutes and you shall keep My judgements and do
them. Then you shall dwell in the land that I gave to your
fathers; you shall be my people and I will be your God.'
                                                    (Ezekiel 36:24-28)

Studying passages like this in the Hebrew prophets
(Jeremiah 30-31, Ezekiel 36-39, Joel 2-3, Zechariah 12-14)
led a number of Christian Bible scholars in the 19th century
to the conclusion that there would be a return to Zion of
the Jewish people in the last days of this age. Among them
was David Baron (1857-1926), who came from Orthodox
Judaism to believe in Jesus as the Messiah. He attended the
first Zionist conference in 1897 and saw there the beginning
of the 'dry bones' of Ezekiel 37 coming together. He believed
that Israel would first be 'born of the flesh' (come into being
as a nation) and then be 'born of the spirit' (experience a
spiritual rebirth).

In the Gospel of John chapter 3 we see the connection with
this passage where Jesus speaks with Nicodemus, a leader of
Israel, about being 'born of the flesh' (natural birth) and being
'born of the spirit' (spiritual rebirth). Jeremiah 31:31-34
prophesies the new covenant through which sin is forgiven
and God's law is written on our hearts. In the New Testament
we see how we can receive this spiritual rebirth through the
new covenant.

According to David Baron the spiritual rebirth of Israel
would come through repentance and faith in Yeshua (Jesus)
the Messiah, not through a return to 'Torah observance'.

Today there are Jewish believers (Messianic Jews) living in Israel who have come to know God through faith in Yeshua. They are often rejected and may face persecution for their faith, but they have the witness in their hearts that they are walking in the truth.

There are a number of prophetic scriptures which indicate a turning to the Lord amongst the Jewish people in the last days. In Revelation 7 we read of 144,000 who are 'sealed' of the tribes of Israel and who bring a huge number of people to the Lord in the first half of the Great Tribulation period. In Revelation 11 we read of the two witnesses who prophesy in Jerusalem and are killed by the Antichrist at the mid point of the Great Tribulation. In Romans 11 we read of the salvation of Israel when:

> 'The Deliverer will come out of Zion, and He will turn away ungodliness from Jacob; for this is My covenant with them when I take away their sins'
>
> (Romans 11:26-27)

This event ties up with Zechariah 12-14 where we read of Israel looking upon *'Me whom they have pierced'* and mourning for Him as for an only son (Zechariah 12:10). Following this, a *'fountain shall be opened for sin and uncleanness'* (Zechariah 13:1). All of this would be fulfilled in an acceptance of Yeshua / Jesus as the Messiah when the Holy Spirit is poured out on the Jewish people in the last days of this age.

5 The Battle for Israel

From the last chapter we should expect to see the following sequence of events taking place regarding Israel:

◊ The Jewish people scattered from the land of Israel and dwelling amongst the Gentile nations of the earth.

◊ The Jewish people keeping their identity in the lands of dispersion and regathering to Israel.

◊ This regathering to be in unbelief.

◊ A time of trouble taking place during which the nations of the world gather against Israel.

◊ Out of this time of trouble a spiritual rebirth to take place as a result of which the remnant of Israel calls on the name of Yeshua (Jesus) for salvation.

◊ The physical return of Jesus the Messiah to the earth to rule and reign from Jerusalem during the Millennium (Messianic Age).

When we look at Jewish history and current events in Israel what do we see? The Jewish people have been scattered to the nations of the world, where for the most part they have been treated shamefully, especially by those who claimed to be Christians. Despite years of oppression in Islamic lands or in Christendom they kept their identity and never lost their desire to go back to the land of Israel. Each year at

Passover they end the meal with the words 'L'shana ha ba b'irushalayim', 'Next Year in Jerusalem.' By such reminders the desire to return to the land of Israel was kept alive through the long years of exile.

According to Ezekiel 36, during the time of this exile the land would become 'desolate wastes' with 'cities that are forsaken' (Ezekiel 36:4). This was exactly the condition Mark Twain, the American author of *Tom Sawyer* and *Huckleberry Finn*, found when he visited Palestine, at that time a backwater of the Turkish Ottoman Empire, in 1867. He described it in his book, *The Innocents Abroad*:

> *'Of all the lands there are for dismal scenery,*
> *I think Palestine must be the prince ... It*
> *is a hopeless, dreary, heart broken land ...*
> *Palestine sits in sackcloth and ashes. Over it*
> *broods the spell of a curse that has withered*
> *its fields and fettered its energies. ... Palestine*
> *is desolate and unlovely.'*

Of Jerusalem he wrote:

> *'Rags, wretchedness, poverty and dirt*
> *abound, lepers, cripples, the blind and the*
> *idiotic assail you on every hand. Jerusalem*
> *is mournful, dreary and lifeless. I would not*
> *desire to live here.'*

By the late 19th century Zionist pioneers, mainly from Russia and Ukraine, began to immigrate into Palestine and to purchase land from absentee Arab landlords. They drained the swamps and planted trees and began the process of turning the barren land into a fertile place. The population of Jerusalem swelled from about 15,000 in 1865 to 45,472 in 1896, of whom 28,112 were Jews. The prophecy of the physical rebirth of Israel was beginning:

*'But you, O mountains of Israel, you shall shoot forth
your branches and yield your fruit to My people Israel,
for they are about to come. For I am indeed for you and
I will turn to you and you shall be tilled and sown. I will
multiply men upon you, all the house of Israel, all of it;
and the cities shall be inhabited and the ruins rebuilt.'*

(Ezekiel 36:8-10)

At around this time the Zionist movement began to organise seriously. At the first Zionist Congress in Basel, Switzerland, Zionist leader, Theodor Herzl, wrote in his diary on August 29th 1897:

*'At Basel I founded the Jewish State. If I were
to say this today, I would be greeted with
universal laughter. In five years, perhaps, and
certainly in fifty, everyone will see it.'*

In November 1917, after the British captured Jerusalem from the Turks, the British government published the Balfour Declaration:

*'His Majesty's government view with favour
the establishment in Palestine of a national
home for the Jewish people, and will use their
best endeavours to facilitate the achievement
of this object, it being clearly understood that
nothing shall be done which may prejudice
the civil and religious rights of existing non-
Jewish communities in Palestine, or the rights
and political status enjoyed by Jews in any
other country.'*

On November 29th 1947, 50 years after Herzl's declaration at the Basel Zionist Congress, the General Assembly of the United Nations passed by 33 votes to 13, with 10 abstentions (including the British), the resolution to partition Palestine, which led to the creation of the State of Israel in May 1948.

Herzl dreamed of an orderly return to Zion from the nations of the world. In fact the return and the establishment of the State of Israel in 1948 came after the agony of the Holocaust and the destruction of one third of the world Jewish population. It also came in the teeth of fierce opposition from the Arab world and from the British government, which had the Mandate for Palestine at that time. Nevertheless the United Nations took the decision to partition Palestine and allow the establishment of a tiny Jewish state on a fraction of the territory originally promised by the British government through the Balfour Declaration.

The immediate and continuing response of the surrounding Arab nations was to seek to eliminate the Jewish state. At times Arab leaders like Nasser of Egypt almost literally quoted the words of Psalm 83:4:

'Come let us cut them off from being a nation, that the name of Israel may be remembered no more.'

In verses 6-8 of this Psalm there is a list of nations, which can be identified with Jordan, Egypt, Lebanon, Gaza, Syria and Iraq. In 1948, 1967 and 1973 Israel had to fight wars for survival against superior armies from these countries bent on pushing the Jewish state into the sea.

In 1964 the Palestine Liberation Organisation (PLO) was set up with the intention of 'liberating' Israeli lands and returning them to Arab control. This was before the Six Day War, which took place in 1967. So the land intended for 'liberation' was the territory of Israel as established in 1948, not the area of the West Bank and Gaza. The Palestine National Covenant, the Charter of the PLO, calls for the 'liberation of Palestine' from the 'Zionist invasion' by 'armed struggle' and 'aims at the elimination of Zionism in Palestine' (i.e. the destruction of Israel). It denies that the Jews are a nation or that they have 'historical or religious ties with Palestine.' It states that only 'the Jews who normally resided in Palestine until the beginning of the Zionist invasion will be considered Palestinians.' Therefore it denies Israel's right to exist in any form and commits the organisation to a programme aiming at the replacement of Israel with a Palestinian State from which the majority of Jewish citizens would be expelled. In pursuing these aims the PLO became the first organisation to use the tactics of modern terrorism, which have been copied by other terrorist organisations throughout the world.

In spite of all that has been thrown against her, Israel has survived and through victories won in 1948 and 1967 ended up with control of more territory than was originally allotted to her by the UN. The Six Day War in 1967 brought the whole of the West Bank (Judea and Samaria), the Golan Heights, the Gaza Strip and the Sinai Peninsula under Israeli control. The West Bank is the name given to the region meaning that it is the west side of the Jordan River, as opposed to the east bank which is the country of Jordan. In August 1967 Israel offered to return these territories in return for peace and recognition by the Arab world, but the response of the Arab nations at the Khartoum Conference was: 'No recognition, no peace, no negotiations with Israel.'

In October 1973 Egypt and Syria attacked Israel on Yom Kippur, the holiest day in the Jewish calendar when Jews fast and pray for forgiveness of sins. For a few days it looked like Israel was about to be overrun by the Egyptians and Syrians, but incredible bravery of Israeli soldiers and God's intervention turned what could have been the end of Israel into another defeat for the Arab armies. In 1979 Israeli Prime Minister, Menachim Begin, and Egyptian President,

Anwar Sadat, signed the Israel-Egypt Peace Treaty which led to the return of the Sinai to Egypt.

For Israel, taking the West Bank meant taking possession of the biblical regions of Judea and Samaria which contain the most significant places in their history from a biblical point of view, including the Old City of Jerusalem and Hebron. From 1948 to 1967 Jerusalem had been a city divided by a wall with barbed wire and checkpoints as Berlin was during the days of the Cold War. The new part of the city, where the Knesset (Israeli parliament) is housed, was under Israeli control. The historic Old City was under Jordanian control. Here were the holy places, sacred to Jews, Christians and Muslims – the Church of the Holy Sepulchre, the Via Dolorosa, the Dome of the Rock and Al Aqsa mosques, (the Temple Mount) and the Jewish Quarter with the Western (Wailing) Wall. During the entire period of Jordanian rule all Jews were expelled from the Old City and unable to pray at the Western Wall.

When the Israelis entered the Old City of Jerusalem on June 7th 1967, the Chief of Staff of the Israeli Defence Force, Moshe Dayan, stood at the Western Wall and said: 'We have regained our holiest place, never again to depart.'

Jewish people worldwide flocked to pray at the Western Wall. The Jewish Quarter of the Old City was resettled with 'yeshivas' (study centres) being established for Orthodox Jews and attracting students from all over the world. At the same time the Dome of the Rock and al Aqsa mosques remain under Muslim control. These mosques stand on the Temple Mount, the site of the Jewish temple in the days of the Bible.

For the Arabs, the establishment of Israel as a Jewish state and Israel's defeat of Arab armies and occupation of Jerusalem and Judea Samaria or the West Bank is a calamity which 'contradicts the march of history'. Jerusalem is considered by Muslims to be the third holiest city in Islam and should be under Arab Muslim control. Indeed the whole of what is called Palestine from the Jordan River to the Mediterranean is regarded as part of the Dar al Islam (house of Islam) and should remain so until the end of days.

The Israeli occupation of the West Bank is also seen as a denial of the Palestinians' right to have a land of their own. So we have today an international effort to make a peace settlement which would hope to resolve the conflict between Israel and the Arab world by Israel withdrawing from territories occupied in the 1967 Six Day War. A Palestinian State should be established and should renounce violence against Israel. At the same time Israel faces implacable hostility from much of the Arab world and from Iran. Iran is allied to Syria and to Hezbollah in Lebanon and Hamas in Gaza and is actively supplying missiles and other weaponry to them.

Peace, Peace

"It is time to put an end to decades of confrontation and conflict and to strive to live in peaceful coexistence and mutual dignity and security." So said Israeli Prime Minister Rabin, as he signed the Oslo Accords with PLO Chairman Yasser Arafat in 1993.

However, even as the agreement was being signed, the leaders were making mutually exclusive claims about Jerusalem. Rabin said, "Jerusalem remains under Israeli sovereignty and our capital." But Arafat said, "Whoever would relinquish an inch of Jerusalem is not an Arab or a Muslim." Seven years later the Oslo Agreement broke down primarily over the issue of Jerusalem. In July 2000 Israeli Prime Minister Barak offered Arafat far more than anyone, including US President Clinton, expected. However Yasser

Arafat refused to compromise over the Palestinian demand for sovereignty over the whole of the Old City of Jerusalem. As this includes the Jewish Quarter and Jewish holy places, there was no way Barak could accept this demand without provoking total rejection from the Israeli population, so bringing down his government. At the meeting of the Islamic Conference Organisation in Morocco a month later in August, Arafat declared: "Our struggle will continue and we won't concede even an inch of the city." Jerusalem remained the 'burdensome stone' just as Zechariah prophesied 2500 years ago.

Since that time the search for a settlement has gone on despite renewed Palestinian violence against Israeli targets unleashed through the Intifada which began in September 2000, the security barrier which Israel erected in order to defend its citizens against terrorist attacks from the Palestinian areas and the split in the Palestinian Authority between the Fatah-led West Bank and Hamas-controlled Gaza.

From 2002 onwards the 'Quartet' of the USA, EU, Russia and UN have been engaged in trying to create some kind of settlement in the Middle East. This means the most powerful nations in the world plus the UN (which represents all nations) are focussed on resolving the status of Jerusalem and of this nation, which is no bigger than Wales. At the time, 2500 years ago, when Zechariah the Hebrew Prophet prophesied that Jerusalem would be a 'burdensome stone' for 'all nations', most people living in Europe, Russia, America would have not known where Jerusalem was, much less been concerned about what was happening there. Today everyone knows where Jerusalem is, and resolving the conflict about who should rule it is top priority for the world powers.

If we fast-forward to the present day, we find that the world is becoming increasingly impatient with Israel for not proceeding to a peace settlement with the Palestinians. The plan is that Israel withdraws from the land it occupied and allows the Palestinians to have an independent state in the West Bank. Then it is claimed that the Arabs will live in peace with Israel.

On March 19th 2010, representatives of the Quartet met in Moscow to issue a statement calling for:

> *'A settlement negotiated between the parties within 24 months, that ends the occupation which began in 1967 and results in the emergence of an independent, democratic, and viable Palestinian state living side by side in peace and security with Israel and its other neighbours.'*

Present at the meeting were U.N. Secretary General Ban Ki-moon, Russian Foreign Minister Sergei Lavrov, US Secretary of State Hillary Clinton, US Special Envoy for Middle East Peace George Mitchell, and High Representative for Foreign Affairs and Security Policy of the European Union Catherine Ashton and Quartet Representative Tony Blair.

So by 2012 the nations of the world want to have the Israel–Palestine issue resolved and a peace settlement in place. However, resolving this issue is not so simple. As far as Israel's Prime Minister Netanyahu is concerned, Jerusalem, the holiest city in the world for Judaism, should remain the undivided capital of Israel. Speaking on Jerusalem Day in May 2009, Israeli Prime Minister Netanyahu said, "United Jerusalem is the capital of Israel. Jerusalem has always been – and always will be – ours. It will never again be divided or cut in half. Jerusalem will remain only under Israel's sovereignty."

As far as the Arab world is concerned, Jerusalem is said to be the third holiest city in Islam, despite the fact that it is never mentioned in the Koran. As such it should be under Arab Muslim control. On 26 April 2009 on America's 'Meet the Press' TV programme, King Abdullah of Jordan said that Israel faces all-out war within 18 months if it does not come to terms with the Arab world and allow the establishment of a new Palestinian state with its capital in Jerusalem. On September 23rd 2010, in his UN General Assembly address, Jordan's King Abdullah again warned that if there was no agreement, a violent conflict could break out.

The Quartet aspires to the creation of 'an independent, democratic, and viable Palestinian state living side by side in peace and security with Israel.' It has to be said that Israel's experience of withdrawing from 'occupied territories' and leaving behind a peaceful democratic neighbour has not been very encouraging so far. In May 2000 Israel withdrew from southern Lebanon ending a 22-year military presence there. The territory was quickly seized by Hezbollah Islamic militants who used it as a base for hostile attacks on Israel with missiles supplied by Iran and Syria. In August 2005 Israel handed over the Gaza strip to the Palestinian Authority, dismantling all its settlements. In June 2007 Hamas took over Gaza and increased the number of missiles fired from its territory into southern Israel.

With this in mind, Prime Minister Binyamin Netanyahu has said that Israel must have a presence in the West Bank to stop rockets from being imported into the area and fired into its territory even after a peace agreement is achieved. The West Bank borders major Israeli cities and is within rocket-firing range of Jerusalem, Tel Aviv and Israel's international airport. Military strategists long have estimated Israel must maintain the West Bank to defend itself from any ground invasion. Hamas leaders have warned they would take over the West Bank as they took over Gaza if Israel pulls out of the territory.

In September 2010 peace negotiations between the Israelis and Palestinians started again in Washington with the aim of finding a settlement within one year. Israeli Prime Minister Benjamin Netanyahu said that he is entering direct peace negotiations with Palestinian Authority President Mahmoud Abbas to find a 'historic compromise' that will enable both people to live in peace for generations. Recalling that after previous Israeli withdrawals from south Lebanon and Gaza, Iran-backed terrorists used those territories to mount attacks on Israel, Netanyahu said it was vital to ensure that any land Israel conceded would not be turned into a 'third Iranian-sponsored enclave aimed at the heart of Israel'. Therefore, the Prime Minister said, a defensible peace required security arrangements that could withstand the test of time.

At the moment of writing (November 2010) the peace talks have been on and off as a result of the issue of Jewish settlements on the West Bank. The Palestinians have said they will not resume talks unless Israel halts the building of Jewish settlements. They want a withdrawal of all Jewish settlements from the West Bank in a final status agreement.

About 500,000 Jews live in settlement blocs and smaller outposts built in the West Bank and East Jerusalem and the surrounding area. Prime Minister Netanyahu supports the settlements in principle. In the 2009 Israeli election he promised to expand Jewish settlements if elected Prime Minister. He also declared that 'Jerusalem is not a settlement', putting Israeli withdrawal from Jerusalem off limits in any final status agreement. Netanyahu's government would fall if he does anything to threaten the future of the Jewish settlers.

This issue more than any other plays into the hands of enemies of Israel and causes Israel to be portrayed as an 'Apartheid state' oppressing the Palestinian people in hostile media. The wall Israel has constructed to prevent attacks

on its territory from Palestinian areas has added to the very
negative image of Israel today. At the time of finishing this
book (November 2010), the question of whether the peace
negotiations with the Palestinians will continue or not depends
on Israel agreeing to freeze on settlement construction.

In previous negotiations Abbas has stated that Israel
must accept all Arab demands. The main ones are a return
to the pre-1967 borders (which means dismantling all the
settlements and dividing Jerusalem) and the right of return
of Palestinian refugees. This would mean that Israel should
open its borders to millions of hostile Arab citizens now
living in Lebanon, Syria and Jordan. This would effectively
mean the destruction of Israel as a Jewish state.

Abbas has consistently refused to recognise Israel as
a Jewish state as Netanyahu has asked him to, saying,
"Historically, there are two states – Israel and Palestine.
Israel has Jews and other people, and this we are ready
to recognize, but nothing else." He has also made it clear
that any future Palestinian State must be 'Israeli free': "We
clarified that the Palestinian Authority would not agree to
continued Israeli presence, military or civil, within a future
Palestinian state."

Abbas has hinted that the Palestinian Authority may
fall apart if the peace negotiations fail. If that happened it
would most likely be replaced by Hamas in power. That
would put an end to any 'peace negotiations', as the Hamas
Charter states:

> *'Israel will exist and will continue to exist until
> Islam will obliterate it, just as it obliterated
> others before it. The Islamic Resistance
> Movement believes that the land of Palestine
> is an Islamic Waqf consecrated for future
> Muslim generations until Judgement Day. It,
> or any part of it, should not be squandered:
> it, or any part of it, should not be given*

*up. There is no solution for the Palestinian
question except through Jihad. Initiatives,
proposals and international conferences are
all a waste of time and vain endeavours.'*

However, it seems that the ultimate aim of the Palestinian
Authority is also the eventual destruction of Israel and its
replacement with a Palestinian State from the Jordan to the
Mediterranean. Even now Palestinian Authority TV, which
is controlled by President Abbas' office, continues to claim
that all of Israel is 'occupied Palestine' and refers to Israeli
cities, including Haifa and Jaffa, as 'occupied Palestinian
cities.' They demand that 'Jerusalem returns to its owners
and we are its owners.'

From Israel's side, Prime Minister Netanyahu has stated
frequently that there should be no return to the 1967 borders
and that Jerusalem should remain the undivided capital of
Israel under Israeli sovereignty. However more recently
Ehud Barak, his Defence Minister, said in response to a
question about the future of Jerusalem:

*'West Jerusalem and 12 Jewish
neighbourhoods that are home to
200,000 residents will be ours. The Arab
neighbourhoods in which close to a quarter
million Palestinians live will be theirs. There
will be a special regime in place along with
agreed upon arrangements in the Old City,
the Mount of Olives and the City of David.
(Ha'aretz newspaper 4/9/10)'*

Does this mean that Israel is now moving to a position
whereby it would accept a division of Jerusalem with some
kind of 'special regime' in the Old City in order to obtain
a peace treaty? Would such a 'special regime' require

some kind of international body to oversee it? Could this be provided by a NATO force policing a peace settlement backed by America, the EU and the UN?

Up until recently the United States has always been seen as being supportive of Israel and its security needs in any negotiations with the Palestinians. However, since Barack Obama became President, there has been a growing tension in this relationship. America wants to mend its relationship with the Arab world and is growing impatient with Israel. Both US and EU leaders have talked of penalising Israel if it does not move ahead with the establishment of a Palestinian state. US special envoy George Mitchell has threatened that his country would freeze its aid to Israel if the Jewish state failed to advance peace talks with the Palestinians and a two-state solution.

During July 2009, the EU's Javier Solana lectured in London and said that if the peace process was going nowhere, the international community should consider recognizing a Palestinian state under a UN resolution even without Israel's consent. European Foreign Ministers have declared their support for the division of Jerusalem, saying that a way should be found to make Jerusalem the shared capital of both Israel and a future Palestinian state. There has even been talk of an international military force being sent into the region to enforce a peace settlement. French President Sarkozy is on record as suggesting placing 40,000 NATO troops in the Palestinian territories to keep the peace.

The Bible prophecies indicate that in the last days a world leader will make a *'covenant'* involving Israel. In Daniel 9 we read about a seven-year covenant made with Israel which breaks down halfway through the seven years and leads to the final time of Jacob's trouble. At the present time we see the attempt to make a peace covenant with Israel with the world powers involved. We also see that the process is continually failing. The end time scriptures indicate that the successful peace covenant will only take place when the Antichrist reaches his seat of power, most likely following the war of Gog and Magog (see following section).

Here is Daniel 9:26-7, with some comments I have added to show this. The passage moves from the time of the Messiah Jesus and His sacrificial death to the last days of this age:

> *'And after the sixty two weeks Messiah shall be cut off but not for Himself;* (i.e. the sacrificial death of the Messiah Jesus) *and the people of the prince who is to come shall destroy the city and the sanctuary* (the destruction of Jerusalem and its Temple in 70AD by the Romans, 40 years after the crucifixion and resurrection of Jesus). *The end of it shall be with a flood and till the end of the war desolations are determined* (following the first coming of Messiah there will be a prolonged period of wars and the desolation of Jerusalem). *Then he* (i.e. the prince who is to come) *shall confirm a covenant* (peace agreement) *with many for one week* (seven years – see Genesis 29:27)*; but in the middle of the week he shall bring an end to sacrifice and offering. And on the wing of abominations shall be one who makes desolate, even until the consummation which is determined is poured out on the desolate.'*

There is a strong emphasis on treachery in the prophecies which surround the last days. *'The treacherous dealers have dealt very treacherously'* (Isaiah 24:16). Concerning the *'prince to come'* Daniel says that *'he shall act deceitfully'* and *'he shall enter peaceably'* even though his real intention is to invade and plunder (Daniel 11:23-4). Leaders of Israel will make a *'covenant with death'* with him and will eventually discover the mistake they have made: *'For we have made lies our refuge and under falsehood we have covered ourselves'* (Isaiah 28:14-15). The peace agreement will break down halfway through the seven-year Great Tribulation period and lead eventually to the final battle for Jerusalem, which will be the occasion for the return of the Lord Jesus to the earth.

War, War

Of course there are also those who want to see Israel removed and replaced by a Muslim state. They show no interest in seeking a peace settlement. Iran's leader, Ahmadinejad, has called Israel a 'stinking corpse' which should be wiped off the map. Iran has been giving support and weapons to Hezbollah in Lebanon and Hamas in Gaza, neither of which have any interest in a temporary peace deal with Israel, but aim at the eventual elimination of Israel and its replacement with a Muslim Arab state, ideally leading to an Islamic Caliphate extending throughout the Middle East. As we have already noted, the Hamas Charter calls for the obliteration of Israel.

By Israel's reckoning, Iran will have the know-how to make nuclear weapons during 2010 and, thereafter, could build atomic bombs within a year. "If Iran gets nuclear weapons, the Middle East will look like hell," says one senior Israeli official. "I cannot imagine that we can live with a nuclear Iran." Ahmadinejad has expressed the hope that even the threat of Iran having a nuclear bomb will cause Jews to leave Israel and therefore bring about the collapse of the State.

Israel also fears the potential of nuclear power in the hands of what it regards as a dangerous 'apocalyptic cult.' According to the leaders of modern Iran we are now living in the last days of this age and the Mahdi will soon appear on the scene. The Mahdi is an Islamic Messiah figure who (it is claimed) will lead the Muslims to defeat 'the Great Satan' (the USA) and the little Satan (Israel) and set up an Islamic world government. According to the Shiite Muslim belief held by Mr Ahmadinejad there will be a time of great trouble on the earth before the Mahdi arrives. In 2008 Ali Larijani, the chairman and speaker of the Iranian Parliament, quoted Imam Mohammed Baqir, a famous Muslim scholar, as saying, "there must be bloodshed and jihad to establish Imam Mahdi's rule." Ayatollah Ibrahim al Amini, professor at the Religious Learning Centre at Qom, stated, "The Mahdi will offer the religion of Islam to the Jews and Christians; if they accept it they will be spared, otherwise they will be killed."

The Islamic Republic of Iran Broadcasting (IRIB) website says the world is now in its 'last days.' It claims that the Mahdi will first appear in Mecca, and then Medina. He will conquer all of Arabia, Syria, Iraq and destroy Israel. Then he will overcome enemies and 'will eradicate all corruption and injustice from the face of the earth and establish the global government of peace, justice and equity.'

Israel faces two bad possibilities in relation to Iran:

◊ Iran gets the bomb and threatens Israel.

◊ Israel attacks Iran's nuclear facilities and faces the consequences of world condemnation and counter attacks from Iran.

In the past Israel has not accepted the risk of a staunch enemy having the means to destroy it. In 1981 Israeli jets destroyed the nuclear reactor being built at Osirak in Iraq before it went operational and began to supply Saddam Hussein with the means to produce a nuclear bomb. In 2007 Israel destroyed a mysterious complex in the Syrian desert widely believed to have been a nuclear reactor being built with help from North Korea.

There have been repeated rumours of Israel staging an attack on Iran's nuclear sites to prevent this from happening. Ehud Barak, Israel's Defence Minister, said in 2009 that a military strike against Iran's nuclear facilities was still an option should the international community fail to put sanctions on Iran tough enough to make it suspend its nuclear programme. Israeli officials estimate that a raid on Natanz and a nuclear facility at Arak, in central Iran, would set Iran's nuclear program back by two to three years.

Such an operation would be far more difficult and dangerous than the raids on Iraq and Syria, given the distances involved, the dispersion of nuclear material at many different sites in Iran, the Iranian air defences and the international repercussions which would follow. Such a raid could provoke a full-scale war between Israel and Iran and its proxies in the region – Syria, Hezbollah in Lebanon and Hamas in Gaza.

On February 27th 2010, Ahmadinejad summoned all the terrorist groups that Iran sponsors for a gathering in Teheran to finalise their roles in military operations against Israel in the event of a Middle East conflagration. He also held talks with Syrian President Bashar Assad and heads of the Lebanese Hezbollah and Palestinian Hamas on February 25th 2010, during a brief visit to Damascus.

In October 2010 Ahmadinejad visited Lebanon and held a massive rally in Bint Jbeil near Lebanon's border with Israel. There he praised the 'resistance' to 'Zionist occupation' and told the cheering crowd that Israel would 'soon evaporate.' Appearing with Hezbollah leaders to whom he has given tens of thousands of rockets and missiles to use against Israel, Ahmadinejad called for them to continue the struggle and promised Iranian 'volunteers' to help fight. Ahmadinejad was greeted as a hero by tens of thousands of Hezbollah members and other Lebanese citizens as he declared his solidarity with them in defiance of Israel. Iranian flags and posters of Ahmadinejad adorned public buildings and lined the streets. A replica of the Al-Aksa Mosque in Jerusalem on the Temple Mount was built in Bint Jbeil, and Iranian flags flew over that as well, a signal many analysts interpreted as a token of a soon coming war.

Iran has provided Hezbollah and Hamas with more than 40,000 rockets and missiles to use against Israel, and Ahmadinejad promised 'volunteers' from the Iranian Revolutionary Guard would come to help in the fight. "The world should know that the Zionists will perish," Ahmadinejad said. "Occupied Palestine will be liberated from the filth of occupation by the strength of resistance and through the faith of the resistance."

In response to this threat, Israel is providing her citizens with masks to defend against weapons of mass destruction. European diplomatic reports have quoted Israeli high ranking officials saying that the Netanyahu government and the Israeli army command are expecting a war against their country waged either jointly by Iran, Hezbollah and the Hamas movement, or by one of these three bodies. There are now tens of thousands of missiles in Lebanon and Syria (on the borders with Israel), mostly supplied by Iran; and Iran itself has long-range missiles capable of reaching Israel.

The Israeli army fears that Hezbollah might launch missiles with biological and chemical warheads capable of reaching Tel Aviv. If this were to happen, Israel confirmed that its response would include targeting southern Lebanon, the suburbs of Beirut and the Bekaa valley. Israel has also let it be known that if Iran strikes Israel with long-range missiles carrying chemical and biological warheads, Israel will respond by devastating air strikes and lethal extremely advanced weapons to target Iranian cities. There are also warnings of Israel and Syria coming to blows, with Israel threatening to attack Damascus if Syria continues to supply Hezbollah with missiles. Syria has said that it would not sit idly by if Israel were to attack Hezbollah in Lebanon.

Israel is also responding to the missile threat by developing anti-missile technology, which is way ahead of anything else in the world. Israel already has the Arrow missile system in place which can detect incoming long-range missiles and shoot them down before they reach Israel. This relies on a directed fragmentation warhead to destroy enemy missiles, a bit like hitting a bullet with a bullet.

In July 2010 Israel successfully test fired the 'Iron Dome' anti-missile system which can intercept short-range missiles coming in from Hamas in Gaza or Hezbollah in Lebanon. An observer who watched this test said:

> *'Iron Dome when faced with a volley of Grad-type Katyushas, fires a counter-volley and the interceptors are required to select and intercept specific Grads in this flying pack. It looked impossible, but they did the impossible. Every missile picked the specific Grad it was asked to select and destroyed it. There's no doubt this is historic.*

(Ha'aretz 21/7/10)'

Israel has also been stocking up on advanced weapons. Given the firepower which is available to Israel, there could also be great destruction on the Arab side. The Hebrew prophet Isaiah prophesied the destruction of Damascus.

This prophecy remains unfulfilled in history. Damascus is the oldest continually inhabited city on earth. Although conquered many times, it has been preserved intact as an economic and cultural centre to this day. But Isaiah predicted Damascus would one day face utter destruction: *"Behold, Damascus is about to be removed from being a city and it will become a fallen ruin"*, he writes in Isaiah 17:1.

From the Bible's point of view all this could find its prophetic fulfilment in Psalm 83 whereby a conflict erupts between Israel and its immediate neighbours resulting in an overwhelming Israeli victory. This is what Psalm 83 says:

> *'O God, do not remain quiet; Do not be silent and, O God, do not be still. For, behold, Your enemies make an uproar; and those who hate You have exalted themselves. They make shrewd plans against Your people, and conspire together against Your treasured ones. They have said, 'Come, and let us wipe them out as a nation, that the name of Israel be remembered no more.' For they have conspired together with one mind; Against You do they make a covenant: The tents of Edom and the Ishmaelites; Moab, and the Hagrites; Gebal, and Ammon, and Amalek; Philistia with the inhabitants of Tyre; Assyria also has joined with them; they have become a help to the children of Lot. Selah.'*

All of these countries surrounding Israel come together with one purpose – to wipe out Israel. There was no historic event in biblical times in which this prophecy has been fulfilled. Certainly we can see elements of its fulfilment in the recent wars of Israel. But could it also have a future fulfilment?

If such a conflict takes place, will Israel survive? Bible prophecy indicates that it will although there may be considerable destruction in the process.

The outcome of this could well be a peace settlement which will hold for a number of years until the next round of conflict is ready with the war of Gog and Magog (Ezekiel 38-9). In this passage an alliance of nations invades Israel led by 'Gog', a leader from the uttermost north of Israel at a time when Israel is at peace in the region. Again this is a prophecy which has never been fulfilled in past events.

'Now the word of the LORD came to me, saying, "Son of man, set your face against Gog, of the land of Magog, the prince of Rosh, Meshech, and Tubal, and prophesy against him, and say, 'Thus says the Lord GOD: "Behold, I am against you, O Gog, the prince of Rosh, Meshech, and Tubal. I will turn you around, put hooks into your jaws, and lead you out, with all your army, horses, and horsemen, all splendidly clothed, a great company with bucklers and shields, all of them handling swords. Persia, Ethiopia, and Libya are with them, all of them with shield and helmet; Gomer and all its troops; the house of Togarmah from the far north and all its troops—many people are with you. Prepare yourself and be ready, you and all your companies that are gathered about you; and be a guard for them. After many days you will be visited. In the latter years you will come into the land of those brought back from the sword and gathered from many people on the mountains of Israel, which had long been desolate; they were brought out of the nations, and now all of them dwell safely. You will ascend, coming like a storm, covering the land like a cloud, you and all your troops and many peoples with you."'*

(Ezekiel 38:1-9)

Joel chapter 2 also speaks of a northern army invading Israel in the last days. Both Joel and Ezekiel 39:1-5, 27-29 show that when this happens God will intervene and destroy this army and that following this there will be an outpouring of the Holy Spirit.

Persia (Iran) is one of the countries mentioned in this war, in which an alliance of nations invades Israel led by 'Gog', a leader from the uttermost north of Israel. Russia, the power to the north, is supplying Iran today with nuclear technology at its Busheir nuclear power station and with advanced weapons. Russia has recently opened up a naval base in Syria. Another country mentioned in the line up of countries taking part in this war is Togarmah which many Bible commentators identify with modern day Turkey. The geographical position of Turkey is significant being the main region of the eastern Roman Empire, which at one time had Constantinople (modern Istanbul) as its capital. Until recently Turkey has been known as a secular Muslim country, seeking membership of the EU and friendly towards Israel, even taking part in joint military exercises with Israel. Now it has become hostile to Israel. Significantly no Arab country bordering on Israel is mentioned in the line up of nations in Ezekiel 38-9.

According to the Bible, the War of Gog and Magog happens after the restoration of Israel from worldwide dispersion and before the end of this age. The nations who take part are supernaturally defeated by God intervening to save Israel. As a result, there is a turning to God in Israel and among the nations.

The final conflict will be the gathering together of the armies of the world (Armageddon) which leads to the physical return of Yeshua / Jesus as King of kings and Lord of lords:

*'And I saw three unclean spirits of demons performing
signs which go out to the kings of the earth and of the
whole earth, to gather them to the battle of that great day
of God Almighty. ... And they gathered them together to
the place called in Hebrew Armageddon.'*

(Revelation 16:13-16)

This time Jesus will not come as a Suffering Servant but
as King of kings and Lord of lords, with all power at His
disposal to rule and reign over the earth. The Hebrew prophet
Zechariah prophesies this event in words which clearly point
to Jesus as the Messiah. He describes a world conflict over
the status of Jerusalem, a question which will not just affect
the countries of the region, but the whole world:

*'And it shall happen in that day that I will make
Jerusalem a very heavy stone for all peoples; and all who
would heave it away will surely be cut in pieces, though
all nations of the earth are gathered against it.'*

(Zechariah 12:3)

When the armies of the world gather together against
Jerusalem to battle, God says:

*'And I will pour on the house of David and on the
inhabitants of Jerusalem the Spirit of grace and
supplication; then they will look on Me whom they have
pierced and mourn for Him as one mourns for his only son.'*

(Zechariah 12:10)

Following this, Zechariah says:

*'Then the Lord will go forth and fight against those
nations, as He fights in the day of battle. And in that day*

His feet will stand on the Mount of Olives, which faces
Jerusalem on the east. ... And the Lord shall be King
over all the earth.'

(Zechariah 14:3-4, 9)

These scriptures point to one who has been 'pierced' as the one who saves Israel in the last days. Who could this be? Yeshua / Jesus, the One who is revealed in the Gospel as the only Son who has been 'pierced', dying by crucifixion, in order to redeem the world, and who will come the second time to judge the world according to how we have responded to His message.

Zechariah 14 is believed by Orthodox Jews to be about the Messiah coming at the end of days and today the Mount of Olives is covered in gravestones. It is the most prestigious place to be buried, because it is believed that the Messiah will come to the Mount of Olives, blow the trumpet for the resurrection of the dead and then those who are buried there will be the first to be resurrected. The theological problem this raises for Orthodox Jews is that if we agree that Zechariah 14 is about the Messiah (and we do!) then the Messiah is called the LORD (Hebrew YHWH – the most sacred name for God). Not only this but He will also apparently have feet and stand on the Mount of Olives. If He has feet presumably He will have the rest of a body as well!

The Mount of Olives is a very significant place in the New Testament also. Jesus gave His teaching on His second coming there (Matthew 24, Mark 13, Luke 21) and ascended into heaven from there. As He did so, an angel spoke to the disciples saying:

This same Jesus who was taken up from you into
heaven, will so come in like manner as you saw Him go
into heaven.'   (Acts 1:11)

The event described in *Zechariah,* when Israel looks on one who has been pierced, will be the same event as the one I have already quoted in Matthew 23:39 when Jesus said concerning Jerusalem:

> *'You shall see Me no more until you say, "Blessed is He who comes in the name of the Lord!"'*

When Jesus is welcomed and accepted as Messiah by the Jewish people, He will come to the earth and finally bring peace to Israel, thus fulfilling the prophecy of Isaiah:

> *'Now it shall come to pass in the latter days that the*
> *mountain of the Lord's house shall be established on*
> *the top of the mountains, and shall be exalted above the*
> *hills; and all nations shall flow to it. Many people shall*
> *come and say, "Come, and let us go up to the mountain*
> *of the Lord, to the house of the God of Jacob; He will*
> *teach us His ways, and we shall walk in His paths." For*
> *out of Zion shall go forth the law, and the word of the*
> *Lord from Jerusalem. He shall judge between the nations,*
> *and rebuke many people. They shall beat their swords*
> *into ploughshares, and their spears into pruning hooks.*
> *Nation shall not lift up sword against nation, neither*
> *shall they learn war anymore.'*

(Isaiah 2:2-4)

SIGNS IN THE WORLD

6   *As in the*
Days of Noah

In 1969, the year before I became a Christian, I was travelling on the London Underground and I looked up and saw a Bible verse posted in one of the ads on the train. I read this:

> *'But know this that in the last days perilous times will come, for men will be lovers of themselves, lovers of money, boasters, proud, blasphemers, disobedient to parents, unthankful, unholy, unloving, unforgiving, slanderers, without self-control, brutal, despisers of good, traitors, headstrong, haughty, lovers of pleasure rather than lovers of God, having a form of godliness but denying its power.'*
>
> (2 Timothy 3:1-5)

As I sat there passing through London's West End, I thought, 'That sounds pretty much like today.' A few months later I became a Christian and now, over 40 years later as I write this book, there is even more evidence that this passage of Scripture applies to our time.

All the prophecies of the Bible tell us that the last days will be 'perilous times' and that there will be great wickedness on the earth. This wickedness will reach its climax in the coming of the one described as the *'Lawless One'* by Paul in 2 Thessalonians 2:

'The coming of the lawless one is according to the working of Satan with all power, signs, and lying wonders, and with all unrighteous deception among those who perish, because they did not receive the love of the truth, that they might be saved. And for this reason God will send them strong delusion that they may all be condemned who did not believe the truth but had pleasure in unrighteousness.'

This coming super wicked man will be empowered by Satan with the ability to deceive people with lying miracles. He is called 'lawless' because he is against God's law as given in the 10 commandments. He is also known as the Antichrist because he is against the Messiah (Christ) Jesus and the good news of salvation through repentance and faith in Jesus. Those who reject this truth will receive the 'strong delusion' offered by the Antichrist. Those who receive the truth and believe in Jesus as Saviour and Lord will be saved.

He is not going to come out of nowhere. In the days which precede the Great Tribulation when the Antichrist appears on the world stage, the world will be prepared for his coming by the spirit of antichrist which will be pervading society. At the same time the Holy Spirit will be gathering together the true believers in Jesus for salvation.

Violence in the Last Days

Jesus spoke of wars in the last days:

'For nation will rise against nation and kingdom against kingdom. And there will be famines, pestilences and earthquakes in various places.'

(Matthew 24:7)

He says that these events will mark the *'beginning of sorrows.'* In other words, the opening shots of the last days' scenario will be characterised by these things happening.

According to information from *Wars and Genocides of the 20th Century* by Piero Scaruffi, (www.scaruffi. com) the 20th century saw conflicts claim around 160,000,000 lives. About 8-9,000,000 died in the First World War and about 55,000,000 in the Second World War. In addition to these there have been civil wars, massacres of people because of racial or religious origin and purges of opponents of totalitarian regimes. Major examples of these are: the Turkish massacre of the Armenians in 1915 (1,200,000 killed), the civil war, purges and conflicts following the Communist revolution in Russia (about 25,000,000 killed between 1917-37), the Nazi Holocaust (6,000,000 Jews plus about 6,000,000 others killed in concentration camps between 1939-45), the partition of India and Pakistan (1,000,000 killed in 1947), the Chinese Communist revolution and subsequent events – Mao's 'Great Leap Forward' and Cultural Revolution – (about 50,000,000 killed between 1946-69), the Korean War and subsequent purges and concentration camps (about 1,600,000 between 1948-94), Nigeria – Biafra civil war (800,000 killed between 1967-70), Pakistan – Bangladesh civil war (500,000 killed in 1971), Ethiopian civil war (1,500,000 killed between 1974-91), Khmer Rouge massacres in Cambodia (1,700,000 killed – about a quarter of the population – between 1975-9), Sudanese civil war (2,000,000 killed between 1983-2000), Rwanda civil war (900,000 in 1994), Yugoslavia's civil war (260,000 between 1992-6), Congo / Zaire war (3,800,000 between 1998 and 2004). All these figures are approximate and, apart from the Congo war, do not include the wars that have taken place since 2000.

The end time prophecies also indicate that in the last days of this age the earth will be full of violence and many people will be afraid of what is going to happen. Jesus said:

'As it was in the days of Noah so will it be in the days of the Son of Man.'

(Luke 17:26-27)

The Bible says that in the days of Noah *'the earth was corrupt before God and the earth was filled with violence'* (Genesis 6:11). In particular there was something happening in the thought life of human beings causing them to act in wicked ways: *'Every intent of the thoughts of his heart was only evil continually'* (Genesis 6:5).

This is certainly what is happening today. TV and films show images of violence and cruelty which people watch every day. Now we have computer games, which glorify aggression and killing. Add to this the influence of drink, drugs, the occult and rock music and you have a potent cocktail leading to violence and uncleanness in human behaviour. Newspapers are full of stories of violent and lawless behaviour in people's homes, in schools and on the streets of our towns and cities. Many people are afraid of going out of their homes after dark.

We see violence taking place in different parts of the world for various reasons. There are conflicts in places where people of different races, tribes or religions live close to each other. There are passages in some religious texts, particularly the Koran, which encourage violence against non-believers. Acts of terrorist violence against western targets or other Muslims are a constant feature of life in some parts of the Muslim world. Christian believers are being targeted for violent persecution in places like Iraq, Egypt and Nigeria, and Iran by Muslims and even by Hindus in parts of India and Buddhists in Sri Lanka. Communist countries like North Korea, China and Vietnam also persecute Christians.

There are many governments which use violence to suppress any opposition to their corrupt rule. The drug trade has been another source of violence with gangs fighting over profits from selling drugs. Also discovery of natural resources often causes violence as greed and big profits cause conflict amongst local people and their exploitation by big business. This has happened in Congo, Africa in particular. Terrorism has affected many areas of the world, as people are encouraged to use force to impose their ideas or religion on others. There are parts of the world where there is regular violence against women, sometimes in the name of religion and sometimes as a result of the sex trade. Even young children are being involved in violent gangs and armed conflicts.

The human race has come a long way from Cain who killed his brother Abel out of jealousy. With all the weapons of destruction available and the images of violence which flash through people's minds on TV screens there is no doubt that we are heading for the end of the age. The way of violence is literally a dead end for many of those who follow it.

By contrast Jesus taught us to seek forgiveness and reconciliation. He said, *'This is My commandment that you love one another as I have loved you.'* (John 15:12)

Sexual Immorality in the Last Days

Along with great violence in the last days the Bible also teaches that there will be a breakdown of family life, and sexual immorality. Jesus said it would be like the days of Lot (Luke 17:28-9). We read about Lot in Genesis 19 where we find him *'sitting in the gate of Sodom.'* Sodom was a wicked city full of sexual immorality with a condition of aggressive homosexuality imposing itself on the rest of society. As a result, '*Lot was oppressed by the filthy conduct of the wicked*' (2 Peter 2:7).

Today we see a worldwide rejection of the Bible's teaching that one man married to one woman is God's will for sexuality, family life and caring for children. All the evidence shows that children brought up in a stable family by their own father and mother have a much better chance in life than those brought up in alternative arrangements.

In much of the world we have easy divorce, multiple sex partners, teenage pregnancies, single parent families and homosexual partnerships being recognised as marriages. There is a huge rise in abortion and sexually transmitted diseases. Child abuse and prostitution have become a global phenomenon, with people travelling around the world to engage in sordid and degrading acts. Much of our popular entertainment is low-level pornography with hard-core porn easily available on the Internet and on cable TV.

We are told that modern attitudes to sex bring freedom and that God's laws are repressive. In fact the opposite is true. Free sex has caused people to be enslaved by destructive habits and desires. Women and children are abused. Because there is no real love and trust, fear and insecurity are the result for all concerned.

The breakdown of the family has left many children with no role models to show them about love and commitment in relationships. This situation can only get worse. Almost half of babies born in England and Wales are born outside of marriage. The British Social Attitudes survey reveals that one in four mothers is now single, up from one in ten 20 years ago. More than half of those have never lived with a man. In most cases the fathers of such children contribute nothing to their welfare and the State provides.

Young people are under constant pressure from the media, teen magazines and even the educational system, to experiment with sex. A booklet produced by the government-funded FPA group, formerly known as the Family Planning Association, aimed at 13-year-olds asks the question, 'How can I tell if I'm ready for sex?' Intended for use in school, personal, social and health education lessons for 13–16 year-olds, it contains detailed information on sexual practices such as masturbation and advice on 'how to be good at sex'. Never mind that it is illegal to have sex under 16! Contraception is easily available and now the 'morning after' contraceptive pill (which is really an abortion pill) is available. Sexually transmitted diseases, many of which lead to infertility, are now rampant among the young.

The *Daily Telegraph* (23/11/05) featured an article 'Sex lessons – do you know what your children are being taught?' It described the 'Personal, social and health education' (PSHE) lessons in King's Manor School in Shoreham, Sussex. Parents were outraged to find out that lessons for 12-year-olds taught about anal, oral and digital sex. The *Daily Mail* (9/3/10) reported that a mother took her seven-year-old daughter out of school after she was made to watch a cartoon showing a couple chasing each other around a bed and having sex. Seven- and eight-year-old pupils watched the controversial Channel 4 sex education DVD, *Living and Growing*, at their village primary school. A voice-over on the DVD describes the sex as 'exciting'. Thousands of the Channel 4 sex education packs have been sold to primary schools across the country.

In America the same story is being told. The *Washington Times* (10/8/09) carried an article entitled: 'You're Teaching My Child What? How To Save Your Family from Sex Ed.' According to the article, 'Much of what is being taught to our young girls and boys in sex education classes is too graphic and vulgar to be quoted in the newspaper. Sex education programmes instruct our children on how to perform sexual acts, including homosexuality and sadomasochism.'

The United Nations is advising governments all over the world to give explicit sexual information to children as young as five. The UN Economic, Social and Cultural Organisation issued its recommended sex education curriculum for children aged 5 to 18. The UN recommends that 5 to 8 year-olds learn about self-gratification and gender violence. The guidelines recommend teaching 9-year-olds the 'safety of abortion, the positive and negative effects of aphrodisiacs, and about homophobia, transphobia, and abuse of power.' 15 year-olds would learn their right to, and access to, safe abortion. Family Therapist Dr. Linda Mintle commented:

> *'This is not so much about educating children on sexual issues. It's really a political ideology that is being forced onto these kids without parents understanding what is happening under the guise of sex education. I think that's very harmful.'*

This sex education concentrates on self-gratification and refuses ever to condemn any form of personal behaviour no matter how destructive. Brenda Almond writes in the *Daily Mail* (25/2/10):

> *'You might say this politically correct, non-judgemental attitude has in fact become the new secular religion of our times with any attempt to raise issues of morality now regarded as a form of heresy.'*

This new secular religion is profoundly anti-Christian and means that there is no right and wrong and that no one should say that there are commandments given by God which should be obeyed. God's commandments are given for our good to prevent us from going down the path to self-destruction. The family is designed by God to be the self-supporting basic building block of society. Children need a father and a mother to look after them and to be a role model and a guide. Once the State becomes provider and arbiter of what is right and wrong, the next step will be for it to become dictator. When the State-run education service actively corrupts its children with amoral sex education, that State is heading for the judgement of God.

We also find that in much of the western world those who question and oppose sexual immorality, and particularly homosexual practice, are being set up for persecution. The European Parliament passed a resolution which calls for abortion rights and 'gay marriage' to be promoted throughout the EU. The resolution calls on all EU member states to recognise same-sex civil partnerships equally with heterosexual marriage and calls for critics to be silenced. The resolution says the European Parliament 'takes the view that discriminatory comments against homosexuals by social and political leaders fuel hatred and violence, and calls on the relevant governing bodies to condemn them.' What does it mean by 'discriminatory'? Those who say that homosexual acts are sinful?

On October 10th 2009, President Obama addressed the largest rally of the US LGBT community (Lesbians, Gays, Bisexuals and Transsexuals). Obama noted that when they look back over the years of his administration, they will "see a time in which we as a nation finally recognized relationships between two men or two women as just as real and admirable as relationships between a man and a woman". Obama also made it no secret that he wants to go beyond policy changes and change hearts. "There are still fellow citizens, good and decent people who hold fast to outworn arguments and old attitudes who fail to see your families like their families", he said. 'Outworn arguments' presumably are to be found in Bible passages like Leviticus 20:13: *'If a man lies with a male as with a woman, both of them have committed abomination'*, or Romans 1:27, which describes homosexual acts as *'shameful'*.

A US judge has overturned California's ban on homosexual marriage after claiming that it was discriminatory and unconstitutional. Proposition 8 was passed by voters in a referendum in 2008 which banned homosexual marriage by amending the California constitution which stated that 'only marriage between a man and a woman is valid or recognised in California'. In making this ruling Judge Vaughn Walker, who is himself homosexual, condemned religious objections to homosexual marriage as both harmful and irrational. The judge stated: 'Gender no longer forms an essential part of marriage; marriage under law is a union of equals.' This has been described as the most controversial re-definition of marriage seen in a Federal Court in the United States, overturning the accepted belief of all religions and cultures up to now that marriage is a union of a man and a woman.

Christian writer Albert Mohler described this ruling as 'a huge win for the homosexual community, and a significant step toward the full normalisation of homosexuality within the culture.'

All three leaders of political parties in Britain expressed their support of the homosexual agenda ahead of the British election in 2010. Meanwhile the House of Lords voted on March 2nd 2010 to change the law on civil partnerships, allowing them to be performed in churches with religious language. The Church of England's governing body has passed a motion in favour of giving civil partners of deceased gay clergy the same pension rights as heterosexual widows or widowers. In effect this vote gives civil partnerships the same status as marriage in the eyes of the Church.

Very few people dare to oppose these developments because they will be howled down with accusations of intolerance and homophobia if they do. But up until recently it was universally accepted that marriage can only be defined as a union between a man and a woman and that homosexual practice is unnatural and a sin according to the Bible. The idea that 'gay marriage' is equal to a marriage between a man and a woman goes against all logic, even on a biological level. A sexual relationship between a man and a woman is capable of producing children but a homosexual relationship can never do this. Gay 'families' rely on heterosexuals or artificial insemination to produce the children they adopt!

The Bible teaches that all sexual acts outside of marriage are sinful in the eyes of God, but offers forgiveness and a new start to all who repent of their sins and believe the Gospel. However much political and even Church leaders want to get away from the truth, the Lord Jesus Christ defined marriage this way:

> *'Haven't you read that at the beginning the Creator*
> *made them male and female, and said 'For this reason a*
> *man will leave his mother and be united to his wife and*
> *the two will become one flesh'? So therefore they are*
> *no longer two but one. Therefore what God has joined*
> *together let not man separate.'*
> (Matthew 19:4-6 quoting Genesis 1:27, 2:24)

Powerful forces within government, backed by the media, the education system and the liberal churches, are imposing the homosexual agenda. Those who hold the biblical view of marriage and homosexuality are being forced to keep their views out of public life and risk losing their jobs if they speak up for biblical moral values. In the name of tolerance and liberalisation a new form of intolerance is arising whereby it is forbidden to go against the flow of sexual liberalisation. 'Gay rights' trump the rights of Bible believers.

As in the days of Lot, we see homosexuality being imposed on society and a revolt against God's order for marriage and society. This is another sign of the perilous times that are prophesied for the last days when people will be *'lovers of pleasure rather than lovers of God, having a form of godliness but denying its power'* (2 Timothy 3:5).

The Occult

Turn on BBC TV at around 5pm for the children's programme and you are more than likely to find yourself watching a programme which is steeped in an occult or pagan worldview. You can be virtually certain that you will not find anything which reflects a Christian or Biblical worldview. As I was working on this chapter of the book I turned on children's TV at 4.45pm on March 31st 2010 and saw a programme called 'Guardians of the Museum' which had three children being given a 'guided tour' of the British Museum. Contained in the tour were images of the 'Dark Lord' and a game to retrieve turquoise tokens which, if the children were successful, would open them up to see 'The Vision.' They were successful and so held hands in a circle with the lady guiding them round and were transported into ancient China where they encountered an old man about to die and gathering objects around him to take with him as he prepared to take his journey into 'the other world.' Frightening images with demonic-looking faces were appearing, and at this point I turned the programme off. How many children around the country kept watching, I wondered? Imagine the outcry if such a programme was telling children about how they can prepare for life after death through believing in the Lord Jesus Christ who died for their sins and rose again from the dead!

Children's games like 'Dungeons and Dragons' and 'Pokemon' also have openly demonic connections. A toys store has been marketing a Ouija board aimed at children aged 8-14. One child who played the game while at a sleepover with her friends wrote:

> *'It was so fun and mysterious at first. Only when it got later into the night and quiet did we realize what we were doing. I asked the Ouija board a foolish question and I didn't get too much of a good answer. After I asked the question I found it very hard to breathe and I found myself shaking. I felt like I was going to die. I took my friend's inhaler 3 times to calm my breathing and my friend were holding me down. This game is witchcraft, voodoo, black magic and Ouija.'*

She is right that Ouija is witchcraft. It is a way to contact evil spirits, asking the spirit in the glass to communicate answers to questions. This is not a game but a way to bring demons into the lives of those who practise it. The fact that it is being marketed as a game for children shows how far down the road of wickedness our society has gone.

Halloween has opened the floodgates to the occult world with all kinds of demonic activity associated with it on sale in the shops and children being encouraged to put on masks and go round houses doing 'trick or treat.' Some would say it is harmless fun, but the roots of Halloween go back to the pagan festival of Samhain. The online Encyclopaedia Britannica gives details of what happened then:

'Huge bonfires were set on hilltops to frighten away evil spirits.... The souls of the dead were supposed to revisit their homes on this day, and the autumnal festival acquired sinister significance, with ghosts, witches, hobgoblins, black cats, fairies, and demons of all kinds said to be roaming about. It was the time to placate the supernatural powers controlling the processes of nature. Samhain was thought to be the most favourable time for divinations concerning marriage, luck, health, and death. It was the only day on which the help of the devil was invoked for such purposes.'

Harry Potter, Merlin, Buffy the Vampire Slayer, Charmed and Sabrina the Teenage Witch have made pagan spirituality and mythology part of pop culture. Apologists for these kinds of programmes generally say that they have no influence on young people's behaviour or beliefs, but the evidence is to the contrary.

The British 'Pagan Federation' reports that popular forms of occult entertainment 'have fuelled a rapidly growing interest in witchcraft among children.' Though it refuses to admit new members under age 18, 'it deals with an average of 100 inquiries a month from youngsters who want to become witches, and claims it has occasionally been 'swamped' with calls. It is quite probably linked to things like Harry Potter, Sabrina The Teenage Witch and Buffy The Vampire Slayer,' explains the Federation's media officer, Andy Norfolk. 'Every time an article on witchcraft or paganism appears, we had a huge surge in calls, mostly from young girls.' (www.ananova.com 'TV show fuels children's interest in witchcraft')

Rock music is also a huge channel for the occult going right back to the 1960s. Both The Beatles and The Rolling Stones had strong occult connections. One of the Beatles' heroes included on the cover of 'Sgt. Pepper' was the Satanist, Aleister Crowley. The Rolling Stones album 'Their Satanic Majesties Request,' leaves no doubt to their allegiance! Their song 'Sympathy for the Devil' is the official anthem for the Church of Satan. In it Lucifer speaks in the first person and asks sympathy for all who meet him. Lead singer, Mick Jagger, claims that Anton LaVey, the founder of the Church of Satan and author of the Satanic Bible, helped inspire their music!

David Bowie in *Rolling Stone* magazine (12/2/76) stated, 'Rock has always been the Devil's music. I believe rock and roll is dangerous. I feel we're only heralding something even darker than ourselves.' AC/DC's song, *Hells Bells*, has the words: 'I got my bell. I'm gonna take you to hell. I'm gonna get ya, Satan, get ya.' In their song *Highway to Hell* they sing: 'Ain't nothing I would rather do goin' down. My friends are gonna be there too. Hey Satan, paid my dues. I'm on the way to the promised land. I'm on the Highway to Hell.' Iron Maiden sing a song called *The number of the Beast* which contains the lyrics 'The number of the Beast 666, the one for me, the one for you.'

The drug culture is a part of the rock and roll scene. Drugs create an altered state of consciousness into which demons can enter a person's consciousness and take control. In Revelation 9:21, where it speaks of *'sorceries'*, the actual word in Greek is 'pharmakeia' which means drugs. Drug taking and sorcery (occult practice) go together with terrible results for those who practise them. This can also apply to alcohol abuse.

Films are another influence in this direction. Commenting on the hugely popular film *Avatar* Joe Schimmel wrote:

*'The film transports the audience into
another worldly realm where worshipping
a tree and communing with spirits are not
only acceptable; they are attractive. Avatar
is also markedly pantheistic and essentially,
the gospel according to James Cameron. This
pantheistic theme that equates God with the
forces and laws of the universe is outwardly
depicted by the heroes and heroine in the
movie who all worship Eywa, the 'All Mother'
Goddess, who is described as 'a network of
energy' that 'flows through all living things'.
Overall, the movie is strewn with ritualistic
magic, communion with spirits, shamanism,
and blatant idolatry as it conditions the
audience to believe these pagan occult lies.
In addition, the audience is led to sympathize
with the Avatar and even ends up pulling for
him as he is initiated into pagan rituals. Even
the lead scientist becomes a pagan in the end,
proclaiming that she is 'with Eywa, she's real,'
and goes to be with her upon her death.'*

(Avatar and the coming One World Religion)

Hollywood has been a major source of New Age occult
beliefs and spreading a world view which is based on the
pantheistic idea that we are all God and that we need not be
concerned about being obedient or accountable to a personal
God who created the universe. However, it is not only film
directors who are seeking to get the world to embrace the
worship of the earth under the guise of their imaginary
Mother Earth Goddess; it is also the leader of the global
warming movement himself, Al Gore.

In his book, *Earth in the Balance*, Gore suggests that we return to the worship of nature and upholds various nature-worshipping sects and Native American religions as a model:

> This pan religious perspective may prove especially important where our global civilization's responsibility for the earth is concerned. Native American religions, for instance, offer a rich tapestry of ideas about our relationship to the earth. All things are connected like the blood that unites us all.

(Al Gore, Earth in the Balance – Ecology and the Human Spirit, 1992, p.258-9)

Seeking a new age synthesis that combines various occult traditions, Gore favourably quotes the Hindu teaching, 'The Earth is our mother, and we are all her children,' (Ibid. p. 161). Gore goes on to claim that we should seek new insights from goddess worshippers of the past and blames Christianity for its near elimination. He claims that ancient beliefs were based 'on the worship of a single earth goddess, who was assumed to be the fountain of all life and who radiated harmony among all living things. The last vestige of organised goddess worship was eliminated by Christianity.' (Ibid, p. 260)

Gore goes on to declare that we need to find a new nature-based religion and quotes New Age theologian, Teilhard de Chardin, in support of the 'new faith' of the future:

> 'This point was made by the Catholic theologian, Teilhard de Chardin, when he said, "The fate of mankind, as well as of religion, depends upon the emergence of a

*new faith in the future." Armed with such a
faith, we might find it possible to re-sanctify
the earth.*

(Ibid, p. 263)'

Such a new faith sounds like the new world religion of the
Antichrist. Paul writing to the Thessalonians warned of the
coming of the 'Man of Sin', or the Antichrist:

*'Now, brethren, concerning the coming of our Lord
Jesus Christ and our gathering together to Him, we ask
you, not to be soon shaken in mind or troubled, either
by spirit or by word or by letter, as if from us, as though
the day of Christ had come. Let no one deceive you by
any means; for that Day will not come unless the falling
away comes first, and the man of sin is revealed, the
son of perdition, who opposes and exalts himself above
all that is called God or that is worshipped, so that he
sits as God in the temple of God, showing himself that
he is God. Do you not remember that when I was still
with you I told you these things? And now you know
what is restraining, that he may be revealed in his
own time. For the mystery of lawlessness is already at
work; only He who now restrains will do so until He is
taken out of the way. And then the lawless one will be
revealed, whom the Lord will consume with the breath
of His mouth and destroy with the brightness of His
coming. The coming of the lawless one is according to
the working of Satan, with all power, signs, and lying
wonders, and with all unrighteous deception among
those who perish, because they did not receive the
love of the truth, that they might be saved. And for this
reason God will send them strong delusion, that they*

*should believe the lie, that they all may be condemned
who did not believe the truth but had pleasure
in unrighteousness.'*

(2 Thessalonians 2:1-12)

The huge rise in interest in the occult today is preparing the way for the coming Antichrist who will be revealed following the Rapture of the Church and will work signs and lying wonders to convince a deceived multitude that he is God. The way to be delivered from this delusion now is to believe the truth, that Jesus is Lord, the Saviour who died for our sins and rose again from the dead to give eternal life to all who believe in Him.

God was not being a killjoy when He commanded the people of Israel not to get involved with the occult:

*'When you come into the land which the Lord your
God is giving you, you shall not learn to follow the
abominations of those nations. There shall not be found
among you anyone who... practices witchcraft, or a
soothsayer, or one who interprets omens, or a sorcerer,
or one who conjures spells, or a medium, or a spiritist,
or one who calls up the dead. For all who do these things
are an abomination to the Lord.'*

(Deuteronomy 18:9-12)

'Abhor what is evil. Cling to what is good.'

(Romans 12:9)

The Bible shows us that there are only two sources of supernatural power that we can experience on this earth. The first and only reliable source is from God Himself. The second source is from Satan and his demons. There are no other sources! New Age and occult arts deceive people with the idea that there is an 'impersonal neutral cosmic type force' that we can all tap into to draw supernatural power from. Those who open themselves up to this force are really tapping into and drawing supernatural power from demonic spirits who are hiding behind the scenes.

Some of these practitioners believe they are drawing this supernatural power from good spirits who mean them no harm. The Bible tells us that Satan and his demons can appear to us as *'angels of light'* (2 Corinthians 11:14), in other words as good spirits, all with the intention of helping us spiritually grow and progress in this life's journey. The reason that God gives such strict warnings about engaging in any of these occult activities is because these occult activities are 'door openers' to the dark side, to Satan and all of his demons. In order to make any kind of direct contact with demonic spirits, you first have to seek after them.

Once you start playing with Ouija boards and tarot cards, seeking after fortune-tellers and astrology, trying things involved with witchcraft such as trying to cast spells, you have automatically placed yourself into a seeking mode with the dark side. Once you have placed yourself into this seeking mode with the dark side, you have just opened the door, you have just given Satan and demonic spirits legal right to enter your world.

The judgement of God is coming upon the world for its violence, sexual immorality and occultism. In the Book of Revelation we read that when the judgements of God strike the world, the majority of mankind will not *'repent of the works of their hands ... And they did not repent of their murders or their sorceries or their sexual immorality or their thefts'* (Revelation 9:20-21). This scripture indicates that in the last days these things will be rife in the earth, with people being conditioned to behave in this way. If you took murder and violence, sorcery (the occult), sexual immorality and theft (crime) out of popular entertainment today there would not be much left. All of this is bringing the judgement of God upon the world and preparing for the Great Tribulation period.

Only Jesus can deliver us from the power of evil and drive out the demonic power once we have allowed it into our lives. As gross spiritual darkness covers the earth and Satan's plan for the control of humanity reaches its climax, the good news is that God is much greater and His power within those who know Him is greater than all the power of evil in the world. The final conflict between the power of God and the power of Satan will be the Second Coming of Jesus when Satan's forces will be utterly routed at Armageddon. Now is the time to get on Jesus' side if you want to see the really exciting spiritual action!

7 *World Coming Together*

According to the prophecies of the Bible, a series of crises will shake the world in the last days. The problems are caused by human sin – greed, aggression, destruction of the earth, false religions and philosophies. God's solution would be for nations to repent and believe the Gospel. But instead the scriptures indicate that only a remnant among the nations will accept Jesus as the Messiah and the majority will reject Him and come together in an anti-Christian world system.

Psalm 2 opens with the words:

'Why do the nations rage and the peoples plot a vain thing? The kings of the earth set themselves and the rulers take counsel against the Lord and against His anointed (Messiah / Christ), saying, "Let us break their bonds in pieces and cast away their cords from us."'

This messianic Psalm speaks of a rejection of the Lord by the rulers of the nations who do not want to be governed by His commandments. When the Psalmist speaks of breaking their bonds and casting away cords, he is speaking of a loosing from the restraint of God's laws. Interestingly in 2 Thessalonians 2 Paul writes about *'the mystery of lawlessness'* in relation to the coming Antichrist who is described as *'the lawless one'*. These nations mentioned in

Psalm 2 are described as being against (or anti) the Anointed One, so they are 'anti-Messiah' / antichrist. The Psalm goes on to say that the Lord has them in derision, knowing that He will set His King / Son / Messiah on His holy hill of Zion who will rule the nations in the Messianic Kingdom age or Millennium.

The prophecies of Daniel and Revelation indicate that there will be an antichrist world system at the end of this age. Chapters 2 and 7 of Daniel are parallel passages in which God gives insight into the world empires which would follow the Babylonian Empire, which was dominant at the time of Daniel.

In Daniel 2 Nebuchadnezzar, king of Babylon, had a dream of a great image with a head of gold, chest and arms of silver, belly and thighs of bronze, legs of iron and feet partly of iron and partly of clay. The image was struck on the feet with a *'stone cut without hands'* and broken in pieces. The stone then became a *'great mountain and filled the whole earth'*, a picture of the Second Coming of Jesus Christ and the kingdom He will set up on the earth after His return.

In Chapter 7 Daniel himself had a vision of four great beasts: a lion, a bear, a leopard and *'a fourth beast dreadful and exceedingly strong'*. In Daniel's vision the empires would be overthrown by *'One like the Son of Man, coming with the clouds of heaven'* who would then have an everlasting dominion over *'all peoples, nations and languages'* (Daniel 7:13-14). Jesus quoted this passage, applying it to His Second Coming in Matthew 24:30 and 26:64.

The interpretation of both chapters is that they refer to a succession of empires, the Babylonian, the Medo-Persian, the Greek and the Roman. All these empires would be run by an oppressive political system, which would be under the spiritual power of *'Mystery Babylon the Great'* (Revelation 17:5) and would therefore conflict in some way with the people of God. The fourth beast (Rome) would be different from all the others and would be revived in the last days.

Daniel prophesied that there would arise from *'this kingdom'* (i.e. the revived Roman Empire), a leader who is described as a *'little horn ... speaking pompous words'* (Daniel 7:8), *'a stern faced king who understands sinister schemes'* (Daniel 8:23) and *'the prince who is to come'* (Daniel 9:26). This one will persecute *'the saints of the Most High'* (Daniel 7:25) and will also make some kind of covenant / treaty with many in Israel for *'one week'* (7 years), a covenant which he will break half way through (Daniel 9:27).

His identity is further revealed in the New Testament Book of Revelation where he is called the Beast, who persecutes the saints and brings in the *'abomination of desolation'* (Daniel 11:31, Matthew 24:15-31, Revelation 13). The Book of Revelation, written in the days of the persecution of Christianity by the Roman Empire (Daniel's fourth beast), describes a future beast, whose leader will be given power by *'ten kings'* (Revelation 17:10-13). His rule will be shattered by the Second Coming of the Lord Jesus in power and glory at the end of this age.

Revelation 13 describes how the 'Beast' is given power by the dragon (Satan) in the final period of this age for 42 months (3 ½ years – the last half of the seven year Tribulation period described in Daniel and Revelation). He blasphemes God and makes war with the saints. *'And authority was given him over every tribe, tongue and nation.'* A second Beast, the False Prophet, makes an image to the Beast which people are made to worship half way through the seven-year Tribulation period. He sets up the mark of the Beast system 666, whereby people receive a mark on their right hand or their foreheads without which they cannot buy or sell.

Revelation 17 describes how the Beast comes to power riding a woman known as Mystery Babylon the Great, a false religious system. He is given power by ten kings as in Daniel 7:

'The ten horns you saw are ten kings who have received no kingdom as yet, but they shall receive authority for one hour with the beast. These are of one mind and they will give their power and authority to the beast.'

(Revelation 17:12-13)

The ten kings are also seen as the ten toes on the image of Daniel 2:40-44:

'And the fourth kingdom shall be as strong as iron, inasmuch as iron breaks in pieces and shatters everything; and like iron that crushes, that kingdom will break in pieces and crush all the others. Whereas you saw the feet and toes, partly of potter's clay and partly of iron, the kingdom shall be divided; yet the strength of the iron shall be in it, just as you saw the iron mixed with ceramic clay. And as the toes of the feet were partly of iron and partly of clay, so the kingdom shall be partly strong and partly fragile. As you saw iron mixed with ceramic clay, they will mingle with the seed of men; but they will not adhere to one another, just as iron does not mix with clay. And in the days of these kings the God of heaven will set up a kingdom which shall never be destroyed; and the kingdom shall not be left to other people; it shall break in pieces and consume all these kingdoms, and it shall stand forever.'

These ten kings did not exist as an entity when John was writing Revelation, but they will come into being in the last days of this age. The early church believed that the ten kings would come into being after the fall of the Roman Empire and would then give their power to the Antichrist. Then Christ would return. Obviously we have been here for much longer than the fall of the Roman Empire (476 AD).

However there are some interesting things that come to light when we look at the Roman Empire. In its later years it divided into the western Empire ruled from Rome and the eastern Empire ruled from Constantinople (modern Istanbul). The east – west division has been seen as the fulfilment of the image of the two legs of the image in Daniel 2. Out of the western division of the Roman Empire, the papacy emerged, with the Pope taking one of the titles of the former Roman Emperors 'Pontifex Maximus.' The eastern Roman Empire was ruled by the predominantly Greek speaking Byzantine Empire, which lost ground to the advancing Muslims and eventually fell in 1453 when the Muslim Turks conquered Constantinople and went on to set up the Ottoman Empire in much of the eastern part of the former Roman Empire. The east-west division remains with us today with Roman Catholicism the dominant religion in the west and Islam dominant in the east.

Students of Bible prophecy have long held that in the last days there will be a Revived Roman Empire out of which the Antichrist will arise. Will this come out of the western Roman Empire or the east? Or will it bring together east and west in a world union? Will the Antichrist arise out of Islam or Roman Catholicism? Or a New World Order which brings both together? The passage in Daniel 2 speaks of the ten toes made of iron and the clay being *'partly strong and partly fragile'* and says that they *'do not adhere to one another'* showing that there is a basic instability in this union as it brings together parts which are really incompatible. It will be destroyed by the Second

Coming of Jesus Christ (the stone which smites the image on its toes and then fills the earth).

The European Union and Globalisation

The most obvious candidate for being a Revived Roman Empire is the European Union. In 2009 the EU nations ratified the Lisbon Treaty through which the EU moved a step closer to the goal dreamed by its founders – a Euro state with its own President, foreign minister, laws, currency and flag. This was the end result of a process which began with the Treaty of Rome, signed in 1957, which looked forward to 'an ever closer union among the peoples of Europe'. Since the Treaty of Rome, the EU has added treaty to treaty, gradually taking over the powers of national governments. It has done this stealthily with most people unaware of what is going on to the point that it now decides far more of our laws and how we are governed than any mainstream politician ever dares admit. The Euro-sceptic journalist, Christopher Booker, described this process as 'the most extraordinary slow-motion coup d'état in history'.

Under the Lisbon Treaty power has been given to the EU to make laws regarding public services, law enforcement, immigration, energy, transportation, tourism, sports, culture, public health, the EU budget, climate change, and so on. As it is a 'self amending' treaty new clauses can be added without the need for further EU treaties or referendums (Art. 48 TEU). This opens the floodgates to further powers to be shifted to the EU from national governments. Commenting on the acceptance of the Lisbon Treaty and appointment of the EU President, journalist Peter Hitchens wrote, 'A great grey Tower of Babel reaches up to the sky over Europe, lopsided, full of cracks and likely to collapse in the fullness of time.'

In November 2009 the EU heads of state came together behind closed doors to choose the first President of the EU and its Foreign Minister. They came up with the relatively unknown Belgian, Herman van Rompuy for President and the even more unknown British peer, Baroness Ashton, for Foreign Minister. Interestingly Mr Van Rompuy said, as he accepted the post on 19 November:

> *'2009 is the first year of global governance with the establishment of the G20 in the middle of the financial crisis. ... The climate conference in Copenhagen is another step toward the global management of our planet. ... Our mission is one of hope supported by acts and by deeds.'*

This statement makes it clear that Mr van Rompuy approves of 'global governance'. He identifies two main ways to bring this about – the financial crisis and climate change. The implication is that national governments cannot solve the problems of the world and that we now need an international body with power to make and enforce laws. Significantly Mr van Rompuy has been identified as a frequent attendee at meetings of the globalist organisations, the Bilderberg Group and the Trilateral Committee.

Interestingly the European Union has used symbols which relate to the Book of Revelation and the Antichrist system. Outside the Council of Europe building in Brussels there stands a statue of Europa (a woman) being carried off by a bull, a picture of the Greek myth of the Rape of Europa. In other words it is a woman riding a beast (Revelation 17).

A poster was issued by the European Union, showing the Tower of Babel and carrying the slogan: 'Many tongues, one voice.' In case the point was lost, a crane in the background was shown rebuilding the tower. Above the Tower of Babel were shown the pointed stars of the EU flag, but inverted, as in witchcraft, with the central points downwards. The EU parliament building, which opened in Strasbourg in December 2000, is deliberately modelled on Brueghel's painting of the Tower of Babel. When asked by a secular journalist, "Why the Tower of Babel?" an EU official replied, "What they failed to complete 3000 years ago – we in Europe will finish now."A number of influential politicians have seen the EU as a model for a New Global Order to be set up, based on regional blocks of nations, to face the new world challenges and bridge the gap between poor and rich.

The Club of Rome is a global think tank composed of scientists, economists, businessmen, international high civil servants, heads of state and former heads of state from all five continents, that deals with a variety of international political issues. It was founded in April 1968 and raised considerable public attention in 1972 with its report 'Limits to Growth'. According to this report, the world should be divided into ten regions which should be loosely modelled on the European Union. The original plan, drawn up in 1972, divided the world as follows.

◊ North America

◊ Europe

◊ Japan

◊ Australasia and Pacific region

◊ Russia

◊ South America

◊ Muslim Middle East

◊ Africa

◊ India and region

◊ China

Some of the boundaries have changed with recent developments, but the development of this idea can be seen in the modern world. Europe is the most advanced region in terms of integration. Russia has set up a customs union with Belarus and Kazakhstan and is seeking to bring Ukraine into this union. In so doing they would succeed in recreating most of the former Soviet Union under Russian domination. China is large enough to constitute a region on its own. Others are moving in the direction of forming unions, some more rapidly, some slowly.

The North American Union is a proposed international body encompassing the nations of Canada, the United States, and Mexico. The blueprint for this governing body was laid out in a 2005 report entitled 'Building a North American Community.'

The Union of South American Nations (UNASUR) was established on May 23rd 2008, with the headquarters to be in Ecuador, the South American Parliament to be in Bolivia, and the Bank of the South to be in Venezuela. The Brazilian President Lula da Silva said that South American nations would seek a common currency as part of the region's integration efforts following the creation of the Union of South American Nations.

Asian nations discussed plans at a major summit to 'lead the world' by boosting economic and political cooperation and possibly forming an EU-style community. The summit groups the 10-member Association of Southeast Asian Nations (ASEAN) with regional partners China, Japan, South Korea, India, Australia and New Zealand.

The African Union was founded in 2002, and is an intergovernmental organisation consisting of 53 African states. At present it is divided: there are those who want to move rapidly towards a united Africa, led by Muammar Ghadaffi of Libya who wants a United States of Africa; but this has been resisted by South Africa and Nigeria, among others, who objected to giving the body too much power at present.

In 2005, the Gulf Cooperation Council (GCC), a regional trade bloc among Bahrain, Kuwait, Oman, Qatar, Saudi Arabia and the United Arab Emirates (UAE), announced the goal of creating a single common currency. It was announced that, 'the region's central bankers had agreed to pursue monetary union in a similar fashion to the rules used in Europe.' Although this region has a relatively small population compared to the others, it has massive wealth due to its oil revenues.

The world is not at the stage yet of creating a world government out of such groupings. Nations still act in their own interests and there remains rivalry between the great powers. There is a growing resistance to globalisation in many parts of the world. Despite this there clearly is a push in the direction of 'global governance' and there are a number of institutions working for this aim. In recent years we have seen world leaders coming together in groups like the G8, G20 and the Davos World Economic Forum to discuss management of the global economy and related issues. We will look at some of these in the next chapter.

An Islamic Union

Many people have pointed out that the EU only occupies one half of the territory of the old Roman Empire. Interestingly Turkey which is very much in the territory of the east Roman Empire has tried to join the EU and thus far has failed to do so. Now it is looking to the east and to its Islamic roots. Recently some in Turkey have even spoken of a revival of the Ottoman Empire to rival the EU.

One of the remarkable features of our time has been the rise of the power of Islam. Since the discovery of oil in the

Middle East and the dependence of the world economic system on the availability of oil, this region has become vitally important to the whole world in modern times. Formerly poor desert regions have become very rich through oil revenues, Saudi Arabia and the Gulf Arab states in particular. These countries are dominated by Islam and have used their wealth to spread the influence of Islam throughout the world. At the same time as the rebirth of Israel in the Middle East, we have seen the renewed power of the Muslim countries of this region. The world's dependence on oil means that no country wants to offend the oil suppliers who for the most part are Islamic.

Some have claimed that the Islamic nations will form the Antichrist power of the last days, even pointing out that there are 10 nations mentioned in Psalm 83 – already quoted in relation to the nations round about Israel that seek to *'cut off Israel from being a nation.'*

Many Muslims believe their time has come and are looking for the world conquest of Islam. A former Jordanian Minister Ali Al-Faqir declared that Islam will conquer Palestine (Israel), Spain and Rome and that America and the EU will soon come to an end:

> *'We must declare that Palestine, from the Jordan River to the Mediterranean Sea, is an Islamic land, and that Spain – Andalusia – is also the land of Islam. Islamic lands that were occupied by the enemies will once again become Islamic. Furthermore, we will reach beyond these countries, which are lost at one point. We proclaim that we will conquer Rome, like Constantinople was conquered once. We will rule the world, as has been said by the Prophet Mohammed.'*

(Memri 2/5/08)

The leaders of the Iranian revolution believe in the coming of the Mahdi, an Islamic Messiah figure who will lead the Muslims to defeat 'the Great Satan' (the USA) and the little Satan (Israel) and set up an Islamic world government. According to the Shiite Muslim belief held by Iran's President Ahmadinejad there will be a time of great trouble on the earth before the Mahdi arrives. The Islamic Republic of Iran Broadcasting (IRIB) website says the world is now in its 'last days.' It claims that the Mahdi will first appear in Mecca, and then Medina. He will conquer all of Arabia, Syria, Iraq and destroy Israel. Then he will overcome enemies and 'will eradicate all corruption and injustice from the face of the earth and establish the global government of peace, justice and equity.'

Libyan leader Ghaddafi said Islam will take over Europe without violent force within a few decades in a speech aired on the Arab satellite network *Al Jazeera* (10/4/06):

> 'We have 50 million Muslims in Europe.
> There are signs that Allah will grant Islam
> victory in Europe – without swords, without
> guns, without conquests. The 50 million
> Muslims of Europe will turn it into a Muslim
> continent within a few decades. Europe is in a
> predicament, and so is America. They should
> agree to become Islamic in the course of time,
> or else declare war on the Muslims.'

This aim was expressed in a document written in 1980 entitled *The Islamic Movement in the West* by Khurram Murad who was then the head of the Islamic Foundation with branches around the world. He outlined his Islamic revolution and the blueprint of how to bring it about in the West. On page three of his document he posed the question: 'What is an Islamic movement?' He goes on to answer: 'An

Islamic movement is an organised struggle to change the existing society into an Islamic society based on the Koran and the Sunna, and make Islam, which is a code for entire life, supreme and dominant.'

Such views can find ample justification in the Koran which teaches that Muslims must be supreme over non Muslims and should be engaged in a jihad to achieve this until the Day of Judgement. 'So lose no heart, nor fall into despair. For you must gain mastery, if you are true in faith. Fight those who believe not in Allah nor the Last Day, nor hold that forbidden which hath been forbidden by Allah and His Messenger, nor acknowledge the religion of Truth, (even if they are) of the People of the Book (i.e. Jews and Christians), until they pay the Jizya (poll tax to be paid by non Muslims living in a Muslim society) with willing submission, and feel themselves subdued.' Sura At-Tawba 9:29 (Yusuf Ali's Translation)

Christian leader, Patrick Sookhdeo has written an article 'The Islamisation of the West' (*Barnabas Aid,* July 2010) in which he shows the means by which this process is going ahead. He writes:

> *'Islamists want Islam to be not just an equal alongside the many other faith communities, but to be privileged and protected. Islamic norms and practices are promoted as Muslims make their presence felt in politics, economics, law, education and the media. ... Islamist movements are dedicated to 'da'wa' (Islamic mission) as part of their attempt to make Islam the dominant religion in the world.'*

Western governments bend over backwards to accommodate Muslim demands, so that now we have halal meat being served in a variety of public places in Britain without any information that this is the case being given to the public. Halal meat, prepared in accordance with Sharia law, requires the cutting of an animal's throat, without stunning the animal first, during which process Islamic verses are recited. We have Muslims in Paris and New York taking over streets for Friday prayers, illegally blocking them to traffic, and the police standing by and allowing this to happen. We have liberal clergymen like the Archbishop of Canterbury proposing that Muslim Sharia law should be permitted to function alongside the law of Britain.

The Organisation of the Islamic Conference (OIC) seeks to give Islam a special place in all societies. They claim that Islam, the Quran, Sharia and Mohammed must all be protected from criticism however factual the criticism may be. Islamist organisations in the West also use laws on libel, human rights and equality to silence any criticism of Islam.

The OIC and its member states are also pressurising other countries at the UN to work on a binding treaty which would protect the religion of Islam from any kind of criticism. The end would be to ban criticism of the beliefs of Mohammed worldwide and therefore outlaw attempts by Christians to show the errors of Islamic beliefs and proclaim that Jesus is the one way to God. In effect this would create a 'global blasphemy law' which would mean that any nation that subscribes to the UN Charter on Human Rights will also have to enforce the blasphemy laws against Mohammed. This could make preaching the Gospel to Muslims illegal according to international law.

Islam certainly has many characteristics of antichrist. After the fall of Communism there has been no other world movement with a stated aim of dominating the world. Muslims in power will not tolerate any opposition to their rule. In the west they are increasingly able to dictate to the rest of society what they want to happen. Generally one does not have to worry too much about making a critical remark about the Pope or Freemasons or New Agers in our society, but if you stand up in public and criticise Mohammed, Islam or Muslims you may well face a death threat.

Whether Islam has the ability to take over Europe, America and the rest of the world is doubtful however. The Muslims themselves are deeply divided along many lines, especially the Sunni – Shiite split. This has led to bloodshed and conflict in Iraq and Lebanon and threatens to destabilise the whole Persian Gulf area. In reality the Sunni regimes of Saudi Arabia and the Gulf Arab states are much more alarmed about Shiite Iran than they are about Israel. Recent revelations have shown that the Saudi king favoured a US military attack on Iran's nuclear facility. Also the threat of Islamist terrorism has made Islam very unpopular in much of the world.

There may be 50 million Muslims in Europe but they are far from being united in the purpose of Islamising Europe. There are those who are moderate and do not wish to live in an Islamised state. We meet many people from a Muslim background in our street evangelism in London who are very negative about Islam. This applies especially to Iranians. The Islamic revolution in Iran has not produced a stable and good society, but a corrupt, incompetent dictatorship. As a result of this there is a great rejection of Islam amongst many Iranians. Many of them are turning to Christ as the answer. Given the opportunity to do so without fear of reprisals, there is no doubt that large numbers would leave Islam if they could. Internet evangelists like Botros Zacharia are winning many Muslims to Christ.

From the point of view of end time prophecy there are aspects of Islam which make it unlikely that it will form the final Antichrist world government. While the Beast of

Revelation 13 does behead his opponents, which is an Islamic practice, he also brings in an act of idolatry, which would be against Islamic teaching. The passage in 2 Thessalonians 2 about the coming Antichrist has him proclaiming himself as God. This would be in direct conflict with the Muslim concept of Allah being totally separate from his creation. In Revelation 13 it is implied that the Beast is initially welcomed as a Saviour figure by the people of the world, whereas radical Islam is seen with fear and hostility by most people in the world. If Islam had world domination it would soon make an end of Israel. The Bible prophecies indicate that despite all the hatred and opposition which Israel receives from Islamic nations and forces it will remain until the end of this age. In fact the defeat of the allied forces of Gog and Magog in Ezekiel 38-9 would include mainly Muslim armies and could result in a shattering of Islamic power and faith.

There is no doubt, however, that Islam and the Middle East will continue to play a major role in the end time scenario of world events. The wealth of the Middle Eastern countries and their oil reserves mean that they will continue to be a powerful force in the coming days. As we shall look at in chapter 12 of this book Islam contains a strong anti-Christian message.

United Nations

Shortly after the First World War, as a result of the Treaty of Versailles in 1919, the League of Nations was founded with the aim of preventing war through collective security, disarmament, and settling international disputes through negotiation and arbitration. It also produced treaties dealing with labour conditions, just treatment of minorities, the arms trade, global health and prisoners of war. This was the first attempt to create a global organisation regulating the behaviour of nations. Its weakness was that, although it could pass resolutions, it lacked the power to enforce them. The rise of aggressive fascist powers in Europe and the Second World War effectively brought an end to the League.

The United Nations replaced it after the end of the Second World War and inherited a number of agencies and organisations founded by the League. The stated aims of the UN are 'facilitating cooperation in international law, international security, economic development, social progress, human rights, and the achieving of world peace'.

As with the League of Nations, one of the issues of the UN has been the lack of power to enforce resolutions and prevent outbreaks of conflict between nations and within nations. A number of influential world politicians and leaders have spoken about the need for some kind of global government which would supersede national sovereignty and deal with global issues such as conflict and disarmament, the environment and financial stability. The aim would be to set up a New World Order:

> *'The New World Order is a world that has a supranational authority to regulate world commerce and industry; an international organisation that would control the production and consumption of oil; an international currency that would replace the dollar; a World Development Fund that would make funds available to free and communist nations alike; and an international police force to enforce the edicts of the New World Order.'*

> *(Willy Brandt, former West German Chancellor and chairman of the Fifth Socialist International in the late 1980's.)*

'This regionalization is in keeping with the
Tri-Lateral Plan which calls for a gradual
convergence of East and West, ultimately
leading toward the goal of one world
government. National sovereignty is no longer
a viable concept.'

(Zbigniew Brzezinski, National Security Advisor to former
US President Jimmy Carter.)

Jan Tinbergen wrote in the 1994 *United Nations Development Report* entitled 'Global Governance for the 21st Century':

'Mankind's problems can no longer be solved
by national governments. What is needed is a
World Government. This can best be achieved
by strengthening the United Nations system.
In some cases, this would mean changing
the role of UN agencies from advice-giving
to implementation.'

The idea behind this is that the world is facing challenges which cannot be solved by individual governments alone – the economic crisis, the environment and the threat of mass destruction from nuclear weapons being the main ones. Those advocating world government are often talking up the threat to human survival. They say that if nothing is done to save us from these threats, then the world faces a calamitous future which could result in the human race being wiped out. This applies especially to the issue of global warming. Many would see a world government with power to enforce decisions on nations and individuals as the only way to deal with this crisis. If we accept that this is the case, then losing some of our freedoms may be seen as a small price to pay.

The UN and organisations like the World Trade Organisation, International Criminal Court, UN peacekeeping force and numerous UN NGO's and other agencies can be seen as the preliminary steps to the formation of a world government. According to an article by George Russell of *Fox News* (September 17th 2010 FoxNews.com) the top leadership of the UN planned to move forward the UN agenda of 'global governance' at a meeting in Austria in September 2010:

> '*With as little public notice as possible, the United Nations Security Council plans to hold a summit meeting to significantly boost its role as a global military and police force, social development agency and international arbitrator, all rolled into one.'*

As one underlying theme of the sessions, the top UN bosses seemed to be grappling often with how to cope with the issue of national sovereignty, which continued to thwart many of their most ambitious schemes, especially when it comes to many different kinds of 'global governance.' The UN would like to see a greater role for itself in 'global governance.' A paper for the first group session of the summit read:

> '*The UN should be able to take the lead in setting the global agenda, engage effectively with other multinational and regional organisations as well as civil society and non-state stakeholders, and transform itself into a tool to help implement the globally agreed objectives.'*

The paper also considers the expansion of the role of UN peacekeepers into a police force operating on the ground in nations.

> '*The UN chiefs also contemplated the further growth of the UN as the world's*

*policeman. As another paper notes, UN
peacekeeping operations "will soon have almost
17,000 United Nations police officers serving
on four continents", little more than two years
after establishing what one papers calls the
institution's "Standing Police Capacity." The
peacekeepers are now also building a "standing
justice and corrections element" to go with
the semi-permanent police force, a permanent
strike force to establish courts and prisons in
nations where peacekeepers are stationed.'*

(September 17th 2010 FoxNews.com).

Another issue of concern to the UN is the security of the
world in the light of the proliferation of weapons of mass
destruction. President Obama gave a speech in Prague in
April 2009 about the need to remove the threat of nuclear
weapons being used. He noted that the threat of all-out
war had gone down with the end of the Cold War but that
the risk of a nuclear attack had gone up as more and more
nations acquire nuclear weapons and the know-how to make
a bomb. He said that terrorists are determined to buy, build
or steal one. Obama went on to speak of the need for all
nations to come together to build a 'stronger, global regime'
to stop the spread of nuclear weapons and to seek the peace
and security of a world without nuclear weapons. He said,
"Some countries will break the rules. That's why **we need a
structure in place** that ensures when any nation does, they
will face consequences."

The dangers posed by nuclear armed 'rogue states' have
heightened with the news, even as I am completing this book,
of an attack by North Korea on a South Korean island. The
Korean Peninsula is potentially one of the most dangerous
regions in the world. At present a mentally unstable dictator

is in possession of nuclear weapons and is threatening his neighbours. The potential to bring the USA and China into the fray is also an ominous part of this equation. Ideally a 'stronger, global regime' would see a change in the North Korean government and its replacement with a unified Korea as part of a Far East regional alliance.

The economic issue, the environment, the spread of nuclear weapons are all issues which are international in nature and threaten the security of the whole world. Pope Benedict XVI has called for a global authority that is able to deal with these issues. His 'Charity in Truth' statement calls for a 'true World Political Authority' to manage the affairs of the world. At the same time, however, the Pope also warns that such an international order could 'produce a dangerous universal power of a tyrannical nature' and must be guarded against somehow. Pope Benedict says this new international order can be accomplished through 'reform of the United Nations Organisation, and likewise of economic institutions and international finance, so that the concept of the family of nations can acquire real teeth.'

If the 'World Political Authority' is to be given 'real teeth' then how are the people of the world going to be able to resist it if it becomes tyrannical? In the end the Antichrist as head of a world political authority with real teeth would seem to be the most likely fit with the prophecies of the Bible.

8 *Financial Crisis*

European President van Rompuy claimed that the financial crisis and the G20 conference held in London in April 2009 was a sign of 'the first year of global governance.' He had good reason for saying this. The financial crisis had the effect of bringing the nations together in conferences aiming at a global solution to a global problem. As events developed in 2008 it became clear that no country could solve the problem on its own. IMF (International Monetary Fund) director, Dominique Strauss-Kahn, described it as a 'global problem which needs a global response.'

It is remarkable to see how many developments are taking place in this direction, especially since the London G20 summit. Not so long ago there was very little contact between countries across the oceans, but now the leaders of Europe, Russia, North and South America, China, India, the Arab world, Africa and Australia come together to try to resolve the crisis affecting all nations.

One of the outcomes of the G20 conference was to issue 'Special Drawing Rights' (SDR), a synthetic paper currency issued by the IMF. Ambrose Evans-Pritchard ran an article in the *Daily Telegraph* (3/4/09) analysing this development:

*'The G20 moves the world a step closer
to a global currency backed by a global
central bank, running monetary policy for all
humanity. ... In effect, the G20 leaders have
activated the IMF's power to create money.
In doing so, they are putting a de facto world
currency into play. It is outside the control of
any sovereign body.'*

On an international level there are fears about the reliability of the dollar as the 'global reserve currency' in view of the massive debts of the US economy. With this in mind many global powers, including Russia, China and India, are proposing a new form of reserve currency. The IMF would like to adopt a plan of action that would expand the use of SDRs (Special Drawing Rights) to replace the US dollar as the global reserve currency and eventually create a global currency called the 'bancor.' The new global currency would be issued by a new global central bank that would have the authority to levy taxes. The bank would have to be accountable to member nations, but remain independent.

The head of the International Monetary Fund, Dominique Strauss-Kahn, has repeated the call for a global currency via SDR multiple times. A UN Report (29/6/10) has also called for abandoning the US dollar as the main global reserve currency, and supported the idea of using the IMF plan. Those opposed to this plan see it as a means of stripping away the sovereignty of nation states and handing economic control of the global economy over to a tiny and potentially despotic ruling elite. The introduction of a new global currency and taxation system, with a regulatory body to oversee it, is a key cornerstone in the move towards global government, centralised control and more power being concentrated into fewer unaccountable hands.

This issue is on the agenda of the G20 group of nations. The G20 is made up of the finance ministers and central bank governors of 19 countries: Argentina, Australia, Brazil, Canada, China, France, Germany, India, Indonesia, Italy, Japan, Mexico, Russia, Saudi Arabia, South Africa, Republic of Korea, Turkey, United Kingdom, United States of America. The European Union, which is represented by the Council President and the European Central Bank, is the 20th member of the G20. The Managing Director of the IMF and the President of the World Bank also participate in G20 meetings.

The G20 describes itself as the 'global premier forum for forging global economic cooperation.' The G20 Summit Preparation Committee has stated:

'The global economy is too closely interwoven to be independent from one another. A nation, or a region, alone cannot work out its own problems. Thus, international cooperation has become indispensible and the role of the G20, as a premier forum for global economic discussions, has significantly grown in importance.'

(Korea IT Times 10/5/10)

Together, member countries represent around 90 per cent of global gross national product, 80 per cent of world trade as well as two-thirds of the world's population.

The G20 report has highlighted the way that the major powers are now dependent on each other. US debt is largely financed by China. China holds about $1.7 trillion in US government debt. The US needs China because of its massive debt. If the US goes down, then the Chinese lose their money. Europe depends on oil and gas from Russia for its energy needs. If the EU goes down, then Russia loses its source of money.

Tal Brooke wrote in his book *When the World will be as One,* page 11:

> *There is the economic call for globalism. Virtually every major name in banking from Rockefeller to Rothschild to Robert McNamara (former president of The World Bank) has spoken of the reality of an interlocking global economy – that what happens on Wall Street one minute is felt in London or Tokyo the next, that the complex jigsaw puzzle of world economy is moving into an oscillating ball that will eventually unify nations and currencies in the global marketplace, and that the economic forces of the earth are moving relentlessly toward a unified world system.*

Such a unified world system would need some kind of government to regulate it.

Financial Crisis and Social Unrest

Economists have called the financial crisis of 2007–2010 the worst financial crisis since the Great Depression of the 1930s. It has left key economies in the world with massive debts, most notably the United States and Britain. The US national debt stands at over $12 trillion at the time of writing (November 2010). It is expanding by about $1 trillion a year. Interest payments on the debt alone came to $452 billion in 2008 and are rising steeply.

Commenting on this, Gary Kah wrote:

*The government only has three options.
It could raise our taxes in order to pay
for these bailouts, which would extract
money from the economy at a time when it
needs more. It could print more currency,
which would lead to hyperinflation and
an eventual collapse. Or, it could borrow
even more from foreign entities – if they
are willing to loan us the money. This
last option would further increase our
colossal debt and lead to our government's
eventual bankruptcy.*

*The fact is our government is almost as
broke as the institutions it is trying to assist.
It is in no position to help. The obvious
next question is, 'Who will bail out the US
Government when it goes broke?' Once
the current system has become completely
undone, I believe a new system will be
proposed as the solution. It will include
some form of global government based on
regional economic arrangements, similar
to the European Union and the proposed
North American Union. Global planners have
long understood there can't be a new one-
world system until the old order has failed.
Developments in the U.S. will most certainly
impact the entire world.*

('En Route to Global Occupation' 10/12/08)

Britain is also badly off. The *Daily Mail* carried an article
by James Palumbo, 'On the brink of financial Armageddon'
(27/11/09). After commenting on Iceland and Dubai
facing bankruptcy without emergency bailouts, he asks
the question:

*'As the country in the world hardest hit
by the credit crunch, with gross domestic
product (GDP) projected to decline by almost
five per cent in 2009, could Britain be next?
We've already had one big shock to Britain's
financial system as many of our best-known
banks teetered on the brink. The Treasury
spent hundreds of billions of taxpayers'
pounds trying to steady the ship. The financial
cupboard is now bare. So what could cause
the second wave of the disaster?'*

He says this could happen as a result of international lenders downgrading the UK's credit rating and dramatically increasing the rates of interest they charge. UK banks will have to follow suit to match these rates, putting unsustainable pressure on our struggling economy:

*'Thousands of businesses already hit by the
recession will go bust. Trapped by soaring
unemployment and welfare benefits, the
Government will have to borrow more. And
so the vicious debt cycle will continue to spiral
down towards national insolvency – and,
potentially, social anarchy.'*

George Osborne, the Chancellor of Britain's new coalition government, has laid out his plans to cut the deficit it inherited from Labour by slashing public spending, leading to job losses and cuts in social services. How this will affect people's lives remains to be seen at the time when this book is being written, but all the pundits are warning of extremely difficult times to come. The opposition to the government is confronted with the argument that if Mr Osborne had not done this, Britain would have lost its AAA credit rating and become bankrupt. In effect this means that international forces are determining the policy of the government. What will happen if this government fails economically as the previous government did?

Trends forecaster Gerald Celente of TrendsResearch. com correctly predicted the collapse of the Soviet Union and the 1997 Asian financial crisis. He now says that the US economy is being propped up by 'phantom money printed out of thin air backed by nothing' which will lead to the decline of America and the possibility of a civil war. The injection of cash into the economy will cause a temporary recovery which will be followed by a crash which will create what he calls the 'Greatest Depression.' Specifically, Celente says the country is headed for rising unemployment, poverty, and violent class warfare as the government efforts to keep the economy going begin to fail. He says that by 2012 there will be 'Food riots, tax protests, farmer rebellions, student revolts, squatter diggins, homeless uprisings, tent cities, ghost malls, general strikes, kidnappings, industrial saboteurs, gang warfare, mob rule, terror.' He sees similar events taking place in Europe.

At the time of completing this book (November 2010) the Euro Zone is in the midst of a major crisis, as Ireland becomes the latest country to need bailing out because of massive debts in its banking sector. Such a bail out has already happened to Greece and may well be needed in Portugal, Spain and possibly Italy. News reports are asking the question, 'Can the Euro survive'? The German leader, Angela Merkel, has warned, 'If the Euro fails, Europe fails.' The consequences of this for the whole of Europe would be incalculable.

So can the Euro (and the EU) fall? Obviously this is a possibility. If it were to happen, it would be impossible to replace national currencies again in a short time and the effect of the fall of the Euro on the economies of Europe would be dire. If this happened it would not just affect Europe. The collapse of a major world currency would affect the global trading system and leave a vital part of that system without a currency to trade with. This would make the 1930s pale into insignificance. Because of this world leaders from America to China and Japan have been urging a solution to the problems of the Euro.

Another basic problem is that there is no mechanism in place for countries that have joined the Euro to leave it, except to leave the EU. If any of the poorer countries in the EU might want to do this, they would be likely to face economic ruin. As soon as they make any move in this direction (for example setting up a means of printing their own currency), investors would withdraw all their money from the banks of the country concerned, with the potential of leaving it bankrupt. Some have speculated that Germany, as the richest country in the Euro region, may want to withdraw from the Euro to avoid having to bail out countries in debt. The problem with this is that if they did so they would lose billions of Euros and immediately put about 3 million people out of work.

The catastrophic potential of all this would be money and savings becoming worthless, mass unemployment, social unrest and possibly even war. To avoid such a crisis the most likely outcome is that European nations will do what is required of them to save the Euro, even if it means handing over more of their sovereignty.

The EU President van Rompuy has spoken of the need to 'strengthen economic governance.' This means control from the centre at the European Council over the governments and economies of the EU. This would be seen as a necessary step to stop the Euro from falling apart. On November 10,

2010, just before departing to Seoul for the G 20 conference, van Rompuy told an audience in Berlin: 'The age of the nation state is over and the idea that countries can stand alone is an 'illusion' and a 'lie.' He equated Euroscepticism with fear, which eventually leads to war – echoing former French president Francois Mitterrand's famous phrase that 'nationalism is war'.

Dominique Strauss-Kahn, the IMF managing director, has said that European nations need to cede more of their sovereignty and hand greater powers to the centre to avoid future crises. In a speech on 22 November 2010 in Frankfurt he called on the European Union to move responsibility for fiscal discipline (i.e. tax raising) and structural reform to a central body that is free from the influences of member states. He said: 'The wheels of co-operation move too slowly. The centre must seize the initiative in all areas key to reaching the common destiny of the union, especially in financial, economic and social policy. Countries must be willing to cede more authority to the centre.'

If this were to happen basically national governments would have to carry out the will of unelected officials of the EU and the European Central Bank. Therefore the current democratically elected governments of individual European nations would become impotent to decide on the economic policy of their own countries. They would become little more than local governments carrying out the will of a central authority which they have no power over.

The EU summit meeting in October 2010 agreed 'to establish a permanent crisis mechanism to safeguard the financial stability of the euro area as a whole and invite the President of the European Council to undertake consultations with the members of the European Council on a limited treaty change required to that effect.' German Chancellor Angela Merkel described the results of this summit as a 'quantum leap' for the stability of the euro. She added that, 'In the future, the Council will now really work as an economic government.'

So the economic crisis could cause the Europeans to unite more. In the process of economic restructuring will they turn over their power to the one known in the Bible as the end time Beast?

Now if someone came along with a plan to rescue the human race from all this, as head of one of the globalist organisations we have looked at in the last chapter, would he not be regarded as the saviour of the world? The Antichrist is the 'man with the plan' who offers peace and safety and a global solution.

Such a man was once called for by Dr. Paul-Henri Spaak, the former Prime Minister of Belgium, also a former Secretary General of NATO and the first president of the United Nations General Assembly. He was instrumental in bringing about the establishment of the European Common Market, the forerunner of the European Union. He said in 1957:

> *'We do not want another committee, we have too many already. What we want is a man of sufficient stature to hold the allegiance of all people, and to lift us out of the economic morass into which we are sinking. Send us such a man, and be he God or devil, we will receive him.'*

In a speech on the 'State of the Union' in Berlin on 8 September 2010 European Commission President Barroso said, 'Europe Needs a Directly Elected Leader with Charisma.'

From Crisis to Dictatorship?

If the social order is threatened, we could see two possible outcomes:

◊ Chaos and anarchy.

◊ Governments bringing in emergency measures to control the population.

The second would seem more likely. Such measures already exist in principle in the US National Security and Homeland Security Presidential Directive signed by President Bush in 2007, which claims power to execute procedures for continuity of the federal government in the event of a 'catastrophic emergency'. Such an emergency is construed as 'any incident, regardless of location, that results in extraordinary levels of mass casualties, damage, or disruption severely affecting the U.S. population, infrastructure, environment, economy, or government functions.' The directive, created by the President, claims that the President has the power to declare a catastrophic emergency. It does not specify who has the power to declare the emergency over.

One could easily see such measures being set up in Russia and China. China remains a one-party Communist state and in Russia the Kremlin owns the majority of the country's economy and resources. This gives the government leverage in controlling the country on every level — socially, politically, economically and financially. In the EU there is the possibility of the whole thing falling apart and reverting to rival squabbling nations as has happened before in European history. But the dangers of this are so great that it is more likely that the EU would become even more of a centrally controlled state as is clearly the wish of those in power in Euroland.

Europol, the police office funded to tackle organised crime in Europe, has already had its powers vastly increased since January 1st 2010 to become the official intelligence gathering arm of the EU and Brussels. The EU now has the power to issue arrest warrants in member countries which can override the legal system of those countries. Civil liberties campaigners have expressed concern over the vague list of 'serious crimes' which the agency can investigate including a person's 'political opinions, religious or philosophical beliefs or trade union membership and data concerning health or sex life.' In a crisis situation this could mean that opposition to EU policies could make an individual liable to arrest. Interest in a person's 'religious beliefs' might also extend to those who think there is a connection between the EU and the Antichrist!

Under the previous government Britain became one of the most spied on nations in the world. According to an article in *The Independent* (26/11/06):

> *'Britain has sleepwalked into becoming*
> *a surveillance society that increasingly*
> *intrudes into our private lives and impacts*
> *on everyday activities. New technology and*
> *'invisible' techniques are being used to gather*
> *a growing amount of information about*
> *UK citizens.'*

This assessment is based on the study 'A Surveillance Society' which predicts that the level of surveillance will grow even further in the next 10 years, which could result in a growing number of people being discriminated against and excluded from society. Future developments could include microchip implants to identify and track individuals; facial recognition cameras fitted into lampposts; and unmanned surveillance aircraft.

This is happening in other parts of the world too. Shenzhen, China's first Special Economic Zone, now has 800,000 surveillance cameras watching Shenzhen's 12 million residents, an average of one camera for every 15 people. According to *Shenzhen Economic Daily*, cameras are systematically installed to monitor city and district borders, main roads and highways, subway stations, government agencies, educational institutions, TV and radio stations, residential areas, and other 'critical' locations. Over 650 other cities in China are also under the close watch of the regime's all-seeing eye.

A means of identifying people through iris and face scanning has been pioneered through a company called Global Rainmakers, Inc (GRI). This has now been set up in the Mexican city of Leon with scanners in place which can identify people as they pass by on the street, and be used to prove identity when withdrawing money from an ATM, getting help at a hospital, and even riding the bus.

An article on the subject appeared on http://singularityhub. com which describes a progamme for biometric ID using iris scanning which has been set up in the Mexican city of Leon:

> *'GRI's implementation in Leon is eventually going to exceed anything we've seen before. Every other means of access (license, credit card, keys, etc) has the potential of being augmented or replaced by iris and face scanning. Get on a bus, pass security on the way into work, pay for a meal, order packages online – all without using anything besides your eye. The Leon project could make this futuristic world appear in just 3 to 5 years. That's incredible. We have to put this in a larger context, too. India just launched*

*its enormous effort to digitally identify more
than a billion residents using fingerprints,
face, and iris scans. Japan already uses finger
scans during entry into the country. The EU
is working on a variety of passive scanning
technologies to help secure airports and other
public spaces.'*

Biometric identification could become mandatory for us all, as Jeff Carter, chief business development officer of GRI, pointed out:

*'When you get masses of people opting-in,
opting out does not help. Opting out actually
puts more of a flag on you than just being
part of the system. We believe everyone
will opt-in.'*

Imagine this kind of technology in the hands of an emerging global government which according to some people is already there waiting in the wings for the moment to take power!

The Cashless Society

While this is happening, there are moves to change permanently the way we buy and sell. The European Commission has produced a report showing the cost of cash to society. It calculated that removing cash and cheques would save the equivalent amount of money as the entire EU agricultural sector. The chequebook is scheduled to be abolished by 2018 after the number issued every day has fallen drastically. The alternative to cheques and cash is the use of electronic cards. More and more transactions are now being made by these cards, with new ones even covering small payments like buying a newspaper or a cup of coffee. Add to this cards used for transport systems like London's Oyster card and you have a growing 'cashless' society.

Visa is now seeking to change the way payments are made for small items such as newspapers and snacks. They believe that contactless cards able to do this will be more widely used. The city of Montpellier in the south of France is offering a glimpse of where this is heading. People there are now able to pay for public transport journeys by waving a memory stick as they enter a bus or tram. The special USB sticks, on sale in the city for €5, can be topped up on line from any computer. The cities of Bordeaux and Toulon have started an experiment in which shoppers can pay through memory sticks for small purchases such as bread, newspapers or cigarettes.

These developments are taking place in Africa as well, where six million people are already paying for goods on their mobiles, proving that electronic payment systems can be more reliable and secure than cash. Ghana is moving to switch the population from using cash with a massive deployment of payment through Point of Sale (POS) machines, which would link the payment systems of all banks, savings and loans as well as rural banks in Ghana. The move means the nation is gradually moving from cash into a cashless society.

The late Bible teacher, Barry Smith, used to say that the 'cashless society' and the use of cards was only the first step towards the ultimate goal of the information in the card being inserted under the skin in a microchip which can be read by Radio Frequency ID scanners and be used to buy and sell. This saves the problem caused by having your card stolen, forged, broken or lost.

He said that this would lead to the Mark of the Beast system of Revelation 13, which describes how the coming

Antichrist or Beast takes over the world by controlling people's ability to buy and sell:

> *'He causes all, both small and great, rich and poor,*
> *free and slave, to receive a mark on their right hand or*
> *their foreheads, and that no one may buy or sell except*
> *one who has the mark of the beast, or the number of his*
> *name. Here is wisdom. Let him who has understanding*
> *calculate the number of the beast, for it is the number of*
> *a man: His number is 666.'*
>
> (Revelation 13:16-18)

It is remarkable that modern technology is doing away with cash and replacing money with electronic devices with which to buy and sell. These involve assigning people with a number which is unique to them and which authorises them to buy and sell. Using such devices also means that someone somewhere knows what you are buying and selling and raises the possibility of monitoring what people are doing and where they are at any given time. It would be possible to cut 'undesirables' off from being able to buy and sell by cancelling their number / card if the people in power choose to do so.

If you put all these factors together, the globalisation of the economy, the financial crisis, the incredible developments of technology and the changes happening already in how we buy and sell, you have the requirements for the Antichrist system described in Revelation 13.

The Bible does speak about a collapse of the global economic system at the end of the Tribulation period when the 'fall of Babylon' will take place in Revelation 18. At this point Babylon is described as a world trading system through which the merchants have become rich:

*'Babylon the great is fallen, is fallen, and has become
a dwelling place of demons, a prison for every foul
spirit, and a cage for every unclean and hated bird! For
all the nations have drunk of the wine of the wrath of
her fornication, the kings of the earth have committed
fornication with her, and the merchants of the earth have
become rich through the abundance of her luxury.'*

(Revelation 18:2-3)

The Book of James also indicates a calamity coming upon
a class of very rich people who will be profiting from the
world economy in the last days and exploiting the majority:

*'Come now, you rich, weep and howl for your miseries
that are coming upon you! You have heaped up treasure
in the last days. Indeed the wages of the labourers who
mowed your fields, which you kept back by fraud, cry
out; and the cries of the reapers have reached the ears of
the Lord of hosts. You have lived on the earth in pleasure
and luxury; you have fattened your hearts as in a day
of slaughter. You have condemned, you have murdered
the just; he does not resist you. Therefore be patient,
brethren, until the coming of the Lord.'*

(James 5:1-7)

9 *Saving the Earth?*

During 2010 we have seen a number of natural disasters. The year began with massive earthquakes in Haiti and Chile, causing huge destruction and loss of life. This was followed by the eruption of Iceland's Eyjafjallajokull volcano which caused billions of dollars in economic damage, and left millions of travellers stranded. Then came the oil spill disaster in the Gulf of Mexico which caused one-third of Gulf waters to be off limits to fishing. Then Pakistan and China were hit by catastrophic flooding bringing massive destruction to life and property and agriculture. At the same time Russia endured a lethal heat wave, causing forests to burn down and crops to be destroyed. Meanwhile in the southern hemisphere's winter unusually cold weather brought snow and ice to much of South America. Now as I finish writing this book unusually cold weather is hitting Britain and much of northern Europe. The weather-related disasters in Pakistan and Russia have raised questions about what is causing this. Meteorologists agree that changes in the Jet Stream have been to blame but this leaves the question, 'Why has this happened?' Is it the result of climate change caused by man-made global warming or is it the result of ocean currents or solar activity which is beyond our control?

According to a report by Charles Hanley for *Associated Press*:

'Scientists point to weather cataclysms as a sign of climate change. Russia's heat wave and wildfires and the record deluge devastating Pakistan fit international scientists' projections of 'more frequent and more intense extreme weather events due to global warming,' according to the World Meteorological Organisation. The U.N.'s network of climate scientists — the Intergovernmental Panel on Climate Change (IPCC) — has long predicted that rising global temperatures would produce more frequent and intense heat waves, and more intense rainfalls. The 2007 IPCC report predicted a doubling of disastrous droughts in Russia this century and cited studies foreseeing catastrophic fires during dry years. It also said Russia would suffer large crop losses.'*

On the other hand, according to Piers Corbyn, a climate change sceptic and astrophysicist of weatheraction.com:

'The superheat and floods in the northern hemisphere and super cold blasts in the southern hemisphere are part of the whole world weather system which is driven by solar-magnetic activity and lunar effects which are predictable months ahead. These extreme weather situations and events, which happen simultaneously around the world, are driven by events on the sun in our predicted Solar Lunar Action Periods (SLAPs). This weather, and climate change, are entirely driven by Solar-Magnetic Lunar effects and are nothing to do with CO_2.'

It makes a big difference who you believe is right in this question. If man-made global warming is the cause then

there may be something we can do about it, but not if it is
the result of events on the sun or the moon.The prevailing
view of the UN and political leaders around the world is
that man-made global warming is responsible for climate
change. Therefore something must be done about it. The
IPCC claims that evidence for warming of the climate is
clear and that the changes are more than 90% likely to
be the result of human actions. It has been claimed that
continuing this process unchecked will cause polar ice to
melt, sea levels to rise, low lying islands and coastal areas
to be flooded, including major cities like London, New
York and Shanghai. Glaciers will melt in the Himalayas
causing sudden floods, followed by drying up of big rivers
on which India, China and other countries depend. There
will be droughts in some places and floods in others. These
claims have all been disputed by climate change sceptics
who say that this is alarmist propaganda which is not
scientifically proven.

To prevent the climate catastrophe scenario, supporters of
the global warming theory have demanded that industrialised
nations make a 20% reduction in carbon emissions by 2020
and 80% by 2050. To achieve this goal, agreements need
to be put in place which will be binding on these nations.
Logically this requires some kind of international authority
to ensure these agreements are kept. In March 2009 Fox
News reported that:

> *'A UN document on Climate Change envisions
> reordering the world economy, likely involving
> trillions of dollars in wealth transfers, millions
> of job losses and gains, new taxes, industrial
> relocations, new tariffs and subsidies, and
> complicated payments for greenhouse gas
> abatement schemes and carbon taxes – all
> under the supervision of the UN.'*

This is not a new idea. In 1974 the Club of Rome produced a report entitled '*Mankind at the Turning Point: The Second Report to the Club of Rome*' stating their desire to create a unified organic (or interdependent) world system. According to the Club of Rome, the world is faced with a set of interlocking world problems, such as over population, food shortages, non-renewable resource depletion and environmental degradation. Left to themselves these problems would lead to the complete unravelling of society and potentially the end of humanity. The solution is some kind of world government.

To this end, Agenda 21 was developed in the United Nation's Earth Summit held in Rio de Janeiro in 1992. This outlines, in detail, the UN's vision for a centrally-managed global society in which governments around the world submit to the United Nation's plan for controlling the way we live, eat, learn, move and communicate – all under the noble banner of saving the earth. To date this has remained a proposal without international agreement to enforce it.

In 2009 the Copenhagen Conference was held in order to secure an international agreement on climate change. UN scientists say that wealthy countries must trim emissions by 25-40% below 1990 levels by 2020 to avoid catastrophic global warming. However, according to the UNFCCC, a UN climate secretariat, the pledges made in Copenhagen will deliver reductions of just 12-18%. This result was a disappointment to environmental activists, especially as the final accord had no reference to a legally binding agreement. Ban Ki-moon, the UN Secretary-General, said, "It may not be everything we hoped for, but this decision of the Conference of Parties is an essential beginning. We must transform this into a legally binding treaty next year."

Other world leaders agreed on the need for a legally binding treaty and committed themselves to work for this in future climate conferences. At the time of writing there is not much progress in this direction, in fact a number of commentators are saying that a global climate deal is further away than ever. One reason for this failure to reach a global climate deal is that nations continue to act in their own interests and politicians do not want to enforce measures which will dramatically reduce the living standards of the people living in their countries. 81% of the world's energy is produced by hydrocarbons (oil, coal and gas) and this energy is currently vital to the economy of the world. So it is hard to see how the targets proposed by the UN can be reached without closing down the economies of much of the developed world. Another reason is a growing scepticism on the subject of climate change after a number of embarrassing errors and exaggerated claims made on the subject by the IPCC and climate scientists.

Added to this is the fear that the climate change issue is being manipulated to impose a dictatorial world government. This claim was made by Lord Monckton (who is a climate change sceptic) in a talk which was broadcast around the world on the Internet. He said that the Copenhagen climate change treaty proposes a world government:

Added to this is the fear that the climate-change isssue is being manipulated to bring a world government. In December 2010 the UN conference on climate change held in Cancún, Mexico, made a formal agreement which committed all countries to cutting emissions for the first time under the UN. This stops short of a legal treaty, but puts in place decisions that will help the world draw up a new treaty in the future. The plan is to bring in this binding treaty at the next UN Climate Conference to be held in Durban, South Africa in 2011.

The final document of the Cancún conference was entitled 'Possible elements of the outcome'. Lord Monckton, a climate-change sceptic, analysed this document. He claims that the huge amounts of money to be channelled into the new UN Fund as a result of this agreement will be used to set up 'a world government directly controlling hundreds of global, supranational, regional, national and sub-national bureaucracies. Hundreds of new interlocking bureaucracies answerable to the world-government Secretariat will vastly extend its power and reach.' Once a 'binding treaty' is set up the nations will be forced to surrender more of their power to this supranational authority. This will be similar to the process that has happened in the various treaties agreed to in the European Union.

Moving towards Revelation 13?

Is global warming real?

The big question raised by all this is whether global warming is a real catastrophe waiting to happen, or a scare story being used by the global elite to bring in their desired global government. Or both? A number of prophetic ministries today dismiss global warming and environmental concerns as a deception to bring in the one world government of the last days.

However we cannot deny that there is a problem about the way the human race is using up the resources of the earth and polluting it in the process. The Bible prophecies indicate that this will be a problem in the last days. There is no question that the rich countries of the world are consuming more food, fuel and other resources that the world can provide without endangering the important ecosystems we all depend on.

Already the world food situation is starting to get very tight. The weather related disasters described at the beginning of this chapter have destroyed crops in Pakistan, China and Russia and there have been locust plagues in Australia and parts of Africa. The world does not grow enough food for everyone and today thousands of people around the world will starve to death. Many agricultural scientists are now warning that global food production is facing dangers that are absolutely unprecedented. The outbreak of a global famine looks increasingly possible with each passing year.

There is no doubt that rapid industrialisation does damage the environment. This is very obviously a problem in China today. Air pollution alone is blamed for hundreds of thousands of deaths each year. Nearly 500 million people lack access to safe drinking water. Only 1% of the country's 560 million city dwellers breathe air considered safe by the European Union. There are industrial cities where people rarely see the sun, children killed or sickened by lead poisoning or other types of local pollution and a coastline so swamped by algal red tides that large sections of the ocean no longer sustain marine life.

In the West industrial society has become ever more dependent on a continuous supply of electricity and oil to maintain our food supply, transport system, computers, cars, televisions and so on. That dependence on fossil fuels causes damage to the environment. A civilisation which depends on fossil fuels to keep its electricity and transport systems going will face enormous changes if we are to reduce carbon emissions at the rate required by climate change agreements. One day we will face this crisis anyway when the coal, oil and gas run out.

Actually a problem in oil supply may not be too far off. Dr Fatih Birol, the chief economist at the respected

International Energy Agency (IEA) in Paris, said that the oil on which modern civilisation depends is running out far faster than previously predicted and that global production is likely to peak in about 10 years – at least a decade earlier than most governments had estimated. He predicts an oil crisis beginning to grip after 2010 and points out that the few countries holding substantial supplies of oil are all located in the unstable Middle East. In this case it is not hard to see restrictions being imposed on our ability to travel – especially by car and by plane – either because of massively rising costs or some form of rationing.

In the 21st Century we rely on oil and gas for transport – cars, lorries, ships, aircraft – as well as electrical power. When the supply of oil and gas runs out, or is restricted by protocols signed to save us from global warming, the great engine of Western civilisation will begin to grind to a halt.

The media is just waking up to the possibility that the lights may start going out all over Britain. Eight of our nine nuclear power stations are reaching the end of their working lives. North Sea gas is running out and we are heading for a 40% shortfall in our energy supplies. EU anti-pollution directives will mean a further nine large coal and oil-fired plants having to close.

The Guardian newspaper reported that the British Department of Energy and Climate Change (DECC) is keeping documents secret which show the UK government is far more concerned about an impending supply crisis than it cares to admit. According to the Guardian, the DECC, the Bank of England and the British Ministry of Defence are working alongside industry representatives to develop a crisis plan to deal with possible shortfalls in energy supply. A leaked report from the Bundeswehr, the German army, has analysed how 'peak oil' might change the global economy. According to the German report, there is 'some probability that peak oil will occur around the year 2010 and that the impact on security is expected to be felt 15 to 30 years later.' The Bundeswehr prediction is consistent with those of well-known scientists who assume global oil production has either already passed its peak or will do so this year.

Bible Prophecies and the Environment

Regarding the environmental issue, there are significant passages which point to natural disasters in the seven-year period of the Great Tribulation which will precede the Second Coming of Christ to the earth. A number of these tie in with conditions being predicted today as a result of climate change.

In Isaiah 24:4-6 we read: 'The earth dries up and withers, the world languishes and withers, the heavens languish with the earth. The earth is defiled by its people; they have disobeyed the laws, violated the statutes and broken the everlasting covenant. Therefore a curse consumes the earth; its people must bear their guilt. Therefore earth's inhabitants are burned up, and very few are left.

Luke 21:25 describes the distress of the nations as *'the sea and the waves roaring.'* This could have a literal application to huge storms or rising sea levels affecting nations. The sea stirred up by the winds is also used in scripture for a picture of humanity in rebellion against God (Isaiah 57:20) so this could also refer to the turmoil caused by the end time crisis.

Revelation 8:7 says, *'A third of the trees were burned up.'* Revelation 16:9 says, *'Men were scorched with great heat.'* Already we are seeing abnormal heat waves causing massive destruction of forests around the world. Also Revelation 16:12 speaks of the River Euphrates being dried up and Isaiah 19:5-10 speaks of the Nile drying up. Since the Nile and the Euphrates are the two great rivers known to the biblical world this could indicate a general drying up of rivers worldwide. Revelation 8:9 says *'A third of the living creatures in the sea died.'*

Jesus also spoke of famines and earthquakes in the last days. *'There will be famines, pestilences, and earthquakes in various places.'* Matthew 24:7. Volcanoes are part of seismic activity and can be included in this sign of the end times. In Revelation 9:2 we read of the plagues that will hit the earth in the time of the Great Tribulation:

> *'And he opened the bottomless pit and smoke arose out of the pit like the smoke of a great furnace. So the sun and the air were darkened because of the smoke of the pit.'*

A number of scriptures speak of the sun being darkened in the Tribulation period. If there was a simultaneous eruption of a number of the earth's 1900 currently active volcanoes it would cause this effect worldwide. So environmental destruction is very much a feature of the last days' scenario according to the Bible.

10 *So What Will Happen to the Nations?*

So far in this book we have looked at current developments taking place in the world. In all these developments there are two common themes:

◊ They tie in with the prophecies of the Bible for the last days of this age.

◊ They are pushing the world in the direction of the time of the Great Tribulation.

Although there have been times of trouble all through history, there will be a unique time of trouble in the days immediately before the Second Coming of Christ to the earth, known as the Great Tribulation. This will be a seven-year period divided in two, so that the final 3½ years will be the most intense time of trouble the world has ever known. The major portion of the Bible which deals with this period is the Book of Revelation, Chapters 6 to 19. These chapters are an expansion of Jesus' teaching on the events preceding His Second Coming to be found in Matthew 24, Mark 13 and Luke 21. Many of the issues dealt with so far in this book are signs that the world is heading towards the Great Tribulation. Following the Rapture of the Church these things will reach their fulfilment.

On the issue of global government, the Bible says that in the last days there will arise a world leader who will be given authority over *'every tribe tongue and nation'* (Revelation 13:7). Known as the Beast or the Antichrist, he will be given power by the Dragon (Satan) and will be aided by one known as the False Prophet, who will work signs and wonders on his behalf. He will be a charismatic figure energised by Satan with supernatural powers (Revelation 13:2-4; 2 Thessalonians 2:9-10). He will offer peace and safety (1 Thessalonians 5:3) but deliver the worst tyranny the world has ever known (Revelation 13).

The book of Revelation indicates that when the time of trouble begins people will divide into two radically different camps.

In Revelation chapter 7 we read of a great harvest of people turning to faith in Jesus at this time, led by Jewish people who supernaturally receive the revelation that Yeshua, Jesus, is the promised Messiah and go out with great power to preach the Gospel in the first half of the Great Tribulation. Because of the insecurity of the time and the fear in the hearts of many people, this will be a very fruitful time for evangelism and as a result a huge number of people will come to faith:

'After these things I looked, and behold, a great multitude which no one could number, of all nations, tribes, peoples, and tongues, standing before the throne and before the Lamb, clothed with white robes, with palm branches in their hands, and crying out with a loud voice, saying, "Salvation belongs to our God who sits on the throne, and to the Lamb!"'

(Revelation 7:9-10)

For the most part these people will be martyred for their faith, as the persecutions of the Great Tribulation get under way:

> *'When He opened the fifth seal, I saw under the altar the souls of those who had been slain for the word of God and for the testimony, which they held. And they cried with a loud voice, saying, "How long, O Lord, holy and true, until You judge and avenge our blood on those who dwell on the earth?"'*
>
> (Revelation 6:9-10)

> *'Then one of the elders answered, saying to me, "Who are these arrayed in white robes, and where did they come from?" And I said to him, "Sir, you know." So he said to me, "These are the ones who come out of the great tribulation, and washed their robes and made them white in the blood of the Lamb"'*
>
> (Revelation 7:13-14)

The majority of people, however, will not turn to Jesus Christ but to Antichrist. At the beginning of the tribulation section of the Book of Revelation we read of the famous 'Four Horsemen of the Apocalypse.'

> *'Now I saw when the Lamb opened one of the seals; and I heard one of the four living creatures saying with a voice like thunder, "Come and see." And I looked, and behold, a white horse. He who sat on it had a bow; and a crown was given to him, and he went out conquering and to conquer. When He opened the second seal, I heard the second living creature saying, "Come and see." Another horse, fiery red, went out. And it was granted to the one who sat on it to take peace from the earth, and that people should kill one another; and there was given*

to him a great sword. When He opened the third seal, I
heard the third living creature say, "Come and see." So
I looked, and behold, a black horse, and he who sat on
it had a pair of scales in his hand. And I heard a voice
in the midst of the four living creatures saying, "A quart
of wheat for a denarius, and three quarts of barley for a
denarius; and do not harm the oil and the wine." When
He opened the fourth seal, I heard the voice of the fourth
living creature saying, "Come and see." So I looked, and
behold, a pale horse. And the name of him who sat on
it was Death, and Hades followed with him. And power
was given to them over a fourth of the earth, to kill with
sword, with hunger, with death, and by the beasts of
the earth'

(Revelation 6:1-8)

These verses show a sequence of events: the conquest of the rider on the white horse, the red horse bringing war, the black horse bringing famine and the pale horse bringing death. This is an overview of the events that are to follow in the Great Tribulation. The question is 'Who is the rider on the white horse?' Some interpreters say this is Jesus riding out to conquer with the Gospel, but there are objections to this view. Firstly Jesus, glorified in heaven, is the one who is revealing these things, not the one being revealed. Secondly what follows the rider on the white horse is war, famine and death, not what one associates with Good News (Gospel means 'good news')!

Thirdly there is an interesting difference between the word for crown in this passage and the word for crown in Revelation 19:12 where the rider on the white horse most definitely is Jesus coming back as King of kings and Lord of lords. In Revelation 19:12 the word is diadem, the crown given from above to one who has royalty. It implies that he is the king by royal status and no matter what opinion anyone else may have of him it does not affect the fact that he is king. This clearly applies to Jesus. In Revelation 6:2, the 'Four Horsemen of the Apocalypse' passage, the crown is the Greek word 'stephanos' which is the kind of crown given by popular approval to a victor at the games, or a victor in battle. This crown is given from below by the people to the man of their choice.

In this case the rider on the white horse is not Jesus Christ, but Antichrist, the one who comes with popular approval with his own agenda and in his own name claiming to be the Messiah for our time. He comes on a white horse indicating two things:

◊ He is a counterfeit Christ or Messiah.
◊ He comes with an offer of peace, which gives him popular approval.

The Antichrist, with the vast communications network of the world at his disposal, will have a power of persuasion backed up by demonic signs and wonders which will dazzle the minds of unbelievers. According to Revelation 13:13 the False Prophet will make *'fire come down from heaven on the earth in the sight of men.'*

The main fear of people alive at this time will be that a world war using weapons of mass destruction will bring about the end of the world. It is likely that the Gog and Magog war of Ezekiel 38-9 will take place first, creating such a fear. Many will turn to the Lord as a result of this event but many others to the Antichrist. The fact that the rider comes on a white horse indicates that he comes with a peace programme, which gives him popular approval. In 1 Thessalonians there is an indication that at this time there is a great 'peace' movement taking place:

'But concerning the times and the seasons, brethren, you have no need that I should write to you. For you yourselves know perfectly that the day of the Lord so comes as a thief in the night. For when they say, "Peace and safety!" then sudden destruction comes upon them, as labour pains upon a pregnant woman.'

(1 Thessalonians 5:1-3)

This global peace movement led by the Antichrist will offer people a false security and will be the reason why he will be accepted as world leader. He will not come conquering by war, but offering what people desperately want – a peace process backed by a global power able to enforce it.

At the moment we see many preparations being made for this. As already stated, the world is coming together in the search for a global solution to global problems. As yet we do not see the UN with the kind of powers necessary to enforce the peace on the world, but we do see progress being made in this direction. We also see nation states surrendering their sovereignty to regional blocs, particularly in the European Union.

The global crisis, which is coming, will speed up this process and it will be presented to the people of the world as the only solution to the threat of mass destruction. People will be persuaded to surrender some personal liberties in order to survive and all the means of communication will be mobilised to put this message across. Dissenting views will be suppressed and the control systems described in Chapter 8 – surveillance equipment, microchips, etc. – will be put to use by the emerging world government to track down opposition to its authority.

The Scriptures indicate that the Antichrist will go forth conquering in the first part of the Great Tribulation and gain control of the world at the mid point of the Great Tribulation period (i.e. after 3½ years). This control will be given to him following an event which will cause the entire world to marvel and follow him:

> *'And I saw one of his heads as if it had been mortally*
> *wounded, and his deadly wound was healed. And all*
> *the world marvelled and followed the beast. So they*
> *worshipped the dragon who gave authority to the beast;*
> *and they worshiped the beast, saying, "Who is like the*
> *beast? Who is able to make war with him?" And he was*
> *given a mouth speaking great things and blasphemies, and*
> *he was given authority to continue for forty-two months.*
> *Then he opened his mouth in blasphemy against God,*
> *to blaspheme His name, His tabernacle, and those who*
> *dwell in heaven. It was granted to him to make war with*
> *the saints and to overcome them. And authority was given*
> *him over every tribe, tongue, and nation. All who dwell on*
> *the earth will worship him, whose names have not been*
> *written in the Book of Life of the Lamb slain from the*
> *foundation of the world. If anyone has an ear, let him hear.*
> *He who leads into captivity shall go into captivity; he who*
> *kills with the sword must be killed with the sword. Here is*
> *the patience and the faith of the saints.'*
>
> (Revelation 13:3-10)

The event which causes this worship of the Beast is 'his deadly wound' being 'healed'. What could this mean? There is much speculation on this but the most intriguing possibility is the one which comes closest to the literal interpretation of the text – that he experiences some kind of death and resurrection by the power of Satan (the Dragon). Since he is a counterfeit Messiah / Christ, what better way to convince the world that he is the Messiah than to counterfeit the resurrection of Jesus?

Whether or not this is the case, the result is clear. He is given power over the nations of the earth. At this point those opposed to him face imprisonment or execution.

The Bible indicates that there will be a great number of people who will turn to Christ in the opening period of the Great Tribulation period. They are encouraged to hold firm to their faith, even if it means losing their lives as a result, because this period of Tribulation is not going to last for long and the end result will be the persecutors being destroyed and the persecuted being saved.

His absolute power lasts for 42 months, which is 3½ years or half of the Great Tribulation period. This is the goal towards which Satan has been working since the Garden of Eden. It will end in total defeat for him and the glorious 1000-year reign of the true Messiah Jesus on the earth, as a prelude to the eternal state in heaven. So the choice before people will be whether they want to be on the side of the loser who will have power for 3½ years or on the side of the winner who will have power for eternity.

The choice will be a hard one for most people to make, because the Antichrist will then bring in a system of control by which people will not be able to buy or sell unless they accept his authority and worship him. In this endeavour he will be helped by a second Beast known as the False Prophet:

'Then I saw another beast coming up out of the earth, and he had two horns like a lamb and spoke like a dragon.
And he exercises all the authority of the first beast in his presence, and causes the earth and those who dwell in it to worship the first beast, whose deadly wound was healed.
He performs great signs, so that he even makes fire come down from heaven on the earth in the sight of men. And he deceives those who dwell on the earth by those signs which he was granted to do in the sight of the beast, telling those

*who dwell on the earth to make an image to the beast who
was wounded by the sword and lived. He was granted
power to give breath to the image of the beast, that the
image of the beast should both speak and cause as many
as would not worship the image of the beast to be killed.
He causes all, both small and great, rich and poor, free
and slave, to receive a mark on their right hand or on their
foreheads, and that no one may buy or sell except one who
has the mark or the name of the beast, or the number of
his name. Here is wisdom. Let him who has understanding
calculate the number of the beast, for it is the number of a
man: His number is 666.'*

(Revelation 13:11-18)

Here we see that the False Prophet will turn the worship of
the Antichrist into a world religion, backed by deceiving
supernatural signs and an act of amazing idolatry. An
image is made of the Beast and people are given the choice
of worshipping this image or being killed. With modern
technology it is not impossible to see how such an image
could be 'given breath' and caused to speak. This act of
idolatry will be coupled with the introduction of worldwide
control of buying and selling. Those who worship the Beast
will receive his mark, the famous 666, without which they
will not be able to buy or sell.

This event will bring about the beginning of the most
terrible time the world has ever known. Revelation 14:9-10
warns the world not to take the mark of the Beast under any
circumstances. Much better to be killed than to take this
mark, which is a sign of submission to Satan and worship of
his man on the earth:

*'Then a third angel followed them, saying with a loud
voice, "If anyone worships the beast and his image,*

*and receives his mark on his forehead or on his hand,
he himself shall also drink of the wine of the wrath of
God, which is poured out full strength into the cup of
His indignation. He shall be tormented with fire and
brimstone in the presence of the holy angels and in the
presence of the Lamb. And the smoke of their torment
ascends forever and ever; and they have no rest day or
night, who worship the beast and his image, and whoever
receives the mark of his name." Here is the patience of
the saints; here are those who keep the commandments of
God and the faith of Jesus.'*

(Revelation 14:9-12)

Following this, the bowl judgements will be poured out on
the earth, leading to the final battle of Armageddon:

*'Then the sixth angel poured out his bowl on the great
river Euphrates, and its water was dried up, so that the
way of the kings from the east might be prepared. And
I saw three unclean spirits like frogs coming out of the
mouth of the dragon, out of the mouth of the beast, and
out of the mouth of the false prophet. For they are spirits
of demons, performing signs, which go out to the kings
of the earth and of the whole world, to gather them to
the battle of that great day of God Almighty. "Behold,
I am coming as a thief. Blessed is he who watches, and
keeps his garments, lest he walk naked and they see his
shame." And they gathered them together to the place
called in Hebrew, Armageddon.'*

(Revelation 16:12-16)

The great Antichrist world government meets its end in most
spectacular style, with the armies of the world gathering
together in the north of Israel in the plains of Megiddo. This

is prior to the final battle which takes place at Jerusalem, culminating in the return of Messiah Jesus to the earth.

Which nations will take part in all this?

In the face of the troubles coming on the world, the prophetic scriptures point to the one world Antichrist system. However there are also passages in Daniel and Revelation which show that this will be unstable and will not hold together.

In Daniel 2 we are shown an image which represents the kingdoms of the world from Daniel's time until the Second Coming of Christ. During the period immediately before that event, there will be a kingdom represented by ten toes of the image, which are:

'partly of iron and partly of clay, so the kingdom is partly strong and partly fragile. As you saw iron mixed with ceramic clay, they will mingle with the seed of men, but they will not adhere to one another, just as iron does not mix with clay.'

(Daniel 2:42-3)

In Daniel 7:24 we read concerning the last days' kingdom that there will be *'ten kings and another shall rise after them. He shall be different from the first ones and shall subdue three kings.'*

Put this together and you have a picture of a 'one world system' in the last days which does not hold together. At some point the world leader will put down or subdue three kings. So there will be some kind of conflict within the one world system, possibly causing one of the wars of the Tribulation period. Finally there will be the great conflict of Armageddon, at which point the Lord Jesus returns to the earth.

It is not possible to see exactly how this will pan out in terms of today's nations or blocks of nations, but certain areas of the world are mentioned in the end time events.

Some form of the European Union is likely to survive all this and emerge as a global power. This may well form the seat of power of the Antichrist. Some students of prophecy have put forward the view that the present EU will morph into something much closer to the exact geographic region of the Roman Empire, which would tie in with the Mediterranean Union I have mentioned previously. This would have its headquarters in Rome rather than Brussels, which is obviously a more significant city! Whether that is the case remains to be seen and I would not rule it out, although I think it is more likely that the present EU will remain and become a much more centralised power than it is today. The EU will be a major player in the attempt to unite the nations economically and socially.

It is hard to find any reference to America in the last days' prophecies, which leads many to believe that the USA will cease to be a great power in the world. Of course America was not on the map as far as the writers of the Bible were concerned so this is not conclusive. It is possible to see the USA as part of the 'revived Roman Empire' since America came out of Europe in the first place. Some would see the USA remaining the leading nation in the 'New World Order' global government. Or it may be that America's massive debt problem, coupled with fatigue at fighting foreign wars in Iraq and Afghanistan, will cause the USA to decline. Plans for a North America Union bringing together the US, Mexico and Canada could mean that America becomes part of another trading block of the world system, with another similar block of nations in South America. Despite all this, I would see America remaining a powerful force in the world, particularly because of its relationship to Israel and its global military reach.

There is a reference which has been attributed to Russia in end time prophecy (Ezekiel 38-9). This suggests that Russia's brief period of democracy is likely to come to an end (some would say it already has done so). A new form of the Soviet Union is already emerging with the customs union that Russia has formed with Kazakhstan and Belarus. Ukraine, and possibly Georgia, will be brought back into the fold as a result of Russian interference in their internal affairs. Russia will use its control over energy and natural resources as a tool to bring neighbouring countries under its sphere of influence. Eventually Russia will break away from the Western-dominated world order and join with Iran, Turkey and other Islamic nations in attacking Israel (Ezekiel 38-9). In this event it will experience the judgement of God and be turned back in defeat. There are those who dispute that this prophecy is about Russia. They say that the nations referred to in Ezekiel 38-9 tie in with the Islamic alliance of nations, principally Iran (Persia), Turkey and Libya, which mount an invasion of Israel in the last days.

China will remain a powerful nation and at the end of this age will send an army of 200 million across the Euphrates into the Middle East. In Revelation 16:12 we are told of the River Euphrates being dried up *'so that the way of the kings of the east might be prepared'*. Revelation 9:14-16 reads:

> *'Release the four angels who are bound at the great river Euphrates." And the four angels who had been kept ready for this very hour and day and month and year were released to kill a third of mankind. The number of the mounted troops was two hundred million. I heard their number.'*

A major social problem China will face, apart from the destruction of the environment, is the imbalance of the ratio of males to females. Because of the 'one child policy' millions of baby girls have been aborted or killed. Between 2000-2004 124 boys were born for every 100 girls in China. Within ten years, China faces the prospect of having the equivalent of the whole young male population of America with little prospect of marriage, untethered to a home of their own and without the stake in society that marriage and children provide.

China's army (the People's Liberation Army, or PLA) has a high number of recruits that are the single child in their family. Quoting *Foreign Policy* magazine, already in 2006 'only-child soldiers made up more than one half of the PLA force, giving China the largest-ever military with a majority of only-children.' With so many single, non-family-rooted men soon coming of military age in the future, events and trends could move into rapid alignment with events prophesied in Revelation 9:14-16.

The Middle East will remain a significant region of the world because of the oil resources of the Gulf region and because of the battle for Israel. As I have already shown, Israel will remain until the Second Coming of Jesus Christ despite repeated attempts to remove her.

In the Book of Zechariah there is a vision of *'a woman sitting inside a basket'* who is identified as *'Wickedness.'* She is carried by a stork (an unclean bird in the Bible) *'to build a house for it in the land of Shinar'* (Zechariah 5:11). Shinar is the area of biblical Babylon, the modern area of Iraq. This is a prophecy of the evil world system which will emerge in the last days of this age, also described in Revelation 18 where it is identified as Babylon the Great. Some have seen a revived Babylon in Iraq as the seat of power of the Antichrist in the last days. Alternatively this prophecy could be applied to the whole region of the Persian Gulf (ancient Babylon) which has become the main exporter of both oil and Islam in our time.

The events I have described in this chapter take place in the Great Tribulation period prophesied in Revelation 6-19. Right now the world situation is preparing the way for these things to happen. Jesus said to those living in the days leading up to this event:

> *'But take heed to yourselves, lest you be weighed down*
> *with carousing, drunkenness, and cares of this life, and*
> *that Day come upon you unexpectedly. For it will come*
> *as a snare on all those who dwell on the face of the*
> *whole earth. Watch therefore and pray that you may be*
> *counted worthy to escape all these things that will come*
> *to pass and to stand before the Son of Man.'*
>
> (Luke 21:34-36)

In the present time the majority of people, including many Christians, are pre-occupied with the pleasures of this life and material things as Jesus indicates here, and are not expecting the Day of the Lord to come in their lifetime. The Great Tribulation period will be a snare to all those who dwell on the earth, because there will be no way out of the troubles that are threatening to bring all life on earth to an end, apart from the intervention of God which will come with the Second Coming of Jesus. The promise to those who *'watch and pray'* is that they will *'escape all these things that will come to pass'*. This is a pointer to the pre-Tribulation Rapture of the Church and an encouragement to us to be ready for this event now.

What is certain from Scripture is that the Lord Jesus will come back to the earth at the end of the Tribulation period with the saints (all those who have believed in Him during this present age). At this point this scripture will be fulfilled:

'The kingdoms of this world have become the kingdoms of our Lord and of His Christ, and He shall reign forever and ever!'

(Revelation 11:15)

He will rule from Jerusalem for 1000 years, during which time Satan will be bound and unable to influence the nations any more. Those who were saved during the Tribulation and martyred for their faith will be resurrected and join in the Messianic Kingdom. This will be the glorious one world government of God when there will be no more war and a renewed and sustainable environment. Then the earth will be filled with the knowledge of the Lord as the waters cover the sea (Isaiah 2:1-4, 11-12, Zechariah 14, Revelation 20).

SIGNS IN THE CHURCH

11 *Persecution of Christians*

|||||||||||||||||||||||||||||||||||||||||||||||||||||||||||||||||||||||||||||||||||||||||||||||||||||||||||||||||

Jesus said that in the days before His coming His followers will be persecuted worldwide:

> *'Then they will deliver you up to tribulation and kill you and you will be hated by all nations for My name's sake.'*
> (Matthew 24:9)

For several years now North Korea has topped the *Open Doors* World Watch List of countries that persecute Christians. It is estimated that there are up to 400,000 to 500,000 believers secretly practising their faith in North Korea. At least a quarter of the Christians are imprisoned for their faith in political prison camps, from which people rarely get out alive, according to an *Open Doors* local source. *Open Doors* ranks eight Muslim countries among the 10 worst persecutors of Christians. The other two, North Korea (which tops the list) and Laos, are communist states. Of the 50 countries on the list, 35 are majority Muslim.

Iran ranks as the world's second-worst persecutor of Christians. *Open Doors* reports that in 2009 the Islamic Republic arrested 85 Christians, many of whom were also mistreated in prison. In 2008, some 50 Christians were arrested and one Christian couple was beaten to death by security officials. At least part of the reason for the mistreatment appears to be the result of Muslim conversions to Christianity: Apostasy carries a mandatory death sentence in Iran.

In Saudi Arabia, all non-Muslim public worship is forbidden. The state forbids the building of any type of non-Muslim house of worship, and Christian expatriates in the kingdom must practise their faith in private. The same goes in the Maldives, where the report notes that all citizens must be Muslim; 'the handful of indigenous Christians are forced to believe in complete secrecy.' Similarly in Mauritania, conversion to Christianity or any other religion is formally punishable by death.

Reports of severe persecution come in regularly from all around the world. Although the situation for Christians in China has improved greatly since the Maoist time, the official government policy is that Christians should worship in the government registered churches of the *Three Self Patriotic Movement* which places them under regulations as to what is acceptable to the Communist state and what is not. Those who do not want to submit to these regulations belong to unregistered 'house churches' which are liable to be closed down at any time.

One of the largest of such house churches is the Linfen Fushan Church in the northern province of Shanxi, with some 50,000 members. In September 2009 police raided the premises where a service was being held and arrested the church's pastor, Wang Xiaoguang. Another ten people were arrested over the following days. Mr Wang and his wife were given the maximum sentence of seven years in prison. The other three people arrested were given sentences of between three and four years. Bob Fu, president of the China Aid Association, said, "This case clearly shows the seriously deteriorating situation of religious persecution in China."

With the fall of Communism, a new day of freedom came for Russia's evangelical Christians. Reports indicate that religious freedom is being squashed again as the government endorses the Russian Orthodox Church as the official state religion and discriminates against other Christian denominations. Protestant churches are required by law to register with the government but, even when the churches register, the government usually finds fault with their paperwork and rejects their applications to be legal bodies of worshippers. There are restrictions on evangelising, and harassment of non-Orthodox worshippers is meant to discourage adherents. In Uzbekistan religions are required to be registered with the government. Christian missionaries are denounced by Islamic theologians as being 'as dangerous as the terrorist activities or the illegal drug trade'. Uzbekistan bans missionary activity and printing of faith-based literature without State consent. This is a pattern which is being repeated in many countries around the world.

In Orissa province of India, a brutal and horrifying persecution in 2008 left many dead and an estimated 50,000 homeless. Hindu extremists blamed Christians for the assassination of anti-Christian Hindu leader Swami Laxamanananda Saraswat, then went on the rampage, torching churches and homes, brutalizing Christians and burning the bodies of those they killed.

In Pakistan Christians face constant harassment by Muslims. Seven Pakistani Christians were burnt alive in the town of Gojra in the Punjab, including three women and two children, when their houses were set on fire during attacks by Muslim demonstrators. Homes were looted and at least 50 houses were burned down, as a Muslim mob threw petrol bombs and fired indiscriminately. The attack was allegedly sparked by rumours that a copy of the Koran had been burned during a Christian wedding. According to eyewitnesses, more than 800 Muslims carrying a variety of weapons raided a Christian settlement. Incited by broadcasts from local mosques, they looted, vandalised and set fire to houses.

There have now been reports of Islamic militants in Pakistan demanding money from non-Muslims in payment of the jizya tax. According to Sharia, this tax is to be imposed on Christians and Jews living in an Islamic state and must be paid as a sign of their submission and lowly status. In Lahore, a letter addressed to a local Christian organisation was handed to a Christian woman by two masked men. The letter said:

> *'We know you are Christian. We warn you to leave this area, embrace Islam, pay 1,500,000 rupees (£10,235; US$18,500; €13,995) as jizya or be ready to die in a suicide attack.'*

Coordinated attacks by Islamic militants in four states of Northern Nigeria left an estimated 80 people dead, including two pastors. At least seven churches are reported destroyed, with other targets, including four police stations, a prison and a customs post. The violence began in Maiduguri, capital of Borno state, on July 26th 2009 when a police station, a prison and five church buildings were set on fire.

In the Middle East, Christians who once played a vital role in their countries are fleeing in droves from persecution and harassment at the hands of Muslims. Political violence and the rise of radical Islam are forcing Christians out of Iraq, Lebanon and Egypt. In the Palestinian Authority-controlled area anti-Christian riots have been reported in Ramallah and surrounding villages as well as in towns in Gaza. Christians have been targeted in scores of attacks, some ending in death. In Bethlehem, local Christians have long complained of anti-Christian violence. The city's Christian population, once 90%, declined drastically since the PA took control in December 1995. Christians now make up less than 25% of Bethlehem, according to Israeli surveys.

A Bible store in the Gaza Strip, the only Christian bookstore in the territory, was attacked by Islamists several times. The store's owner, Rami Ayyad, was found shot dead in 2007, his body riddled with bullets. He was publicly tortured a few blocks from his store before he was killed. The witnesses said they saw three armed men, two of whom were wearing masks, beat Ayyad repeatedly with clubs and the butts of their guns while they accused him of attempting to spread Christianity in Gaza. Sheik Abu Saqer, leader of Jihadia Salafiya, said that Christians could continue living safely in the Gaza Strip only if they accepted Islamic law. He said, "Christian schools and institutions must show publicly what they are teaching to be sure they are not carrying out missionary activity." Abu Saqer accused the leadership of the Gaza Christian community of "proselytizing and trying to convert Muslims with funding from American evangelicals."

The tiny number of ethnic Somali Christians practise their faith in secret under extremely dangerous conditions. At least ten Christians, including four teachers, were killed for their faith in 2008 and several others were kidnapped and raped. Two masked members of the al-Shabaab Muslim militia shot and killed a Christian pastor in Somalia as he drove home from a worship service. An Algerian woman is facing jail for converting from Islam to Christianity and for carrying 10 copies of the Bible on a bus.

These are just a handful of examples of the persecution of Christians which takes place across the Muslim world. Above all, the Muslims want to outlaw any attempts to convert Muslims to Christianity and any negative statements about Mohammed.

The issue of Christian persecution, especially in Muslim lands, is rarely if ever reported in the mainstream news. The BBC falls over itself to highlight any mistreatment of Muslims that may take place, but studiously ignores the massive number of Christians persecuted on a daily basis by Muslims around the world. Tony Blair has called Islam a peaceful religion and President Obama said in his speech in Cairo in June 2009: "Throughout history, Islam has demonstrated through words and deeds the possibilities of religious tolerance and racial equality." Neither Tony Blair nor Barrack Obama produced evidence to back these claims.

Shades of Persecution in the West

But it is not just countries traditionally associated with persecution of Christians where the heat is being turned up.

Public life in Britain under the previous government showed increasing signs of suppression and persecution of anyone who does not toe the line of 'political correctness'. An Australian writer, Hal Colebatch, described Britain as the 'world's first soft totalitarian state' in an editorial in *The Australian* (21/4/09). He says that, while there may as yet be no concentration camps or gulags in Britain, 'there are thought police with unprecedented powers to dictate ways of thinking and sniff out heresy, and there can be harsh punishments for dissent.' He points to the dozens of cases over the last ten years in which Christians and others, who hold traditional moral views, have been targeted by police and other governmental agencies for their beliefs.

In many cases, the threats, firings, suspensions and arrests have targeted Christians who hold traditional social and moral beliefs about sexuality. "Any one of these incidents," he said, "might be dismissed as an aberration, but taken together – and I have only mentioned a tiny sample more are reported almost every day – they add up to a pretty clear picture."

Some victims of the 'thought police' include Duke Amachree, a social worker with the homeless, who discussed his faith with a colleague and was then told it was inappropriate to 'ever talk about God'. He was also told that he may not even say, 'God bless.' His case comes after a number of public sector workers have seen their employers forcing secularist views on them.

Also we are seeing attempts to shut down open air preaching. Two preachers in Manchester read passages from the Bible saying that homosexual sex is sinful. A police officer said that he had received complaints and that reading such passages from the Bible was offensive and could be charged with incitement to homophobia. They were told that they should only read the bits of the Bible that don't offend people. I would not be surprised to see restrictions on open air preaching and distribution of Christian literature in the coming days. One reason for this will be complaints by gay rights groups and religious minorities claiming that they are 'offended' by what the Christians are saying.

Mainstream TV stations consistently ridicule and undermine Christianity. Almost every Christmas and Easter some unbelieving clergyman or atheist will appear on the BBC or Channel 4 to give reasons why the Bible account of the birth or resurrection of Jesus is wrong. Bible believers are never given an opportunity to counter these programmes. At the same time, no one would ever dare question Muslim beliefs at Ramadan or Hindu beliefs at Diwali. Richard Dawkins is regularly given the opportunity to rubbish Bible teaching on Creation, and all nature and scientific programmes assume evolution to be a proven fact. Creationists are coming up with very good reasons to believe the biblical account of creation. They show why the evidence points away from evolution to creation, but they are never given any chance to air their views in the media.

In 2006, executives at the BBC admitted that they would consider broadcasting a scene where the Bible was thrown into a bin but they would never do the same with the Koran. In the same year, the Archbishop of York, Dr John Sentamu, said that Christians took 'more knocks' in BBC programmes than other faiths.

Dr Sentamu said, "They can do to us what they dare not do to the Muslims. We are fair game because they can get away with it."

Former BBC presenter, Don Maclean, has said, "I think there's a secularist movement in this country to get rid of Christianity." Speaking of the BBC he added, "They're keen on Islam, they're keen on programmes that attack the Christian Church."

Richard Littlejohn described the BBC as "riddled with an institutional mindset which holds that it is fine to heap scorn on Christians and Jews but cravenly appeases Muslims at every turn." (*Daily Mail*, 21/8/07)

Even in America there is a rising tide of hostility towards Christians and Christians are finding limits being put on their freedom of speech. A New Mexico judge warned a graduating class that he was sending a US Marshall to their graduating ceremony to ensure that nobody said the name 'Jesus.' A teacher at a school in Houston, Texas, threw away two students' Bibles, calling them garbage. She then took the students to the Principal's office where she threatened to call Child Protection Services onto their parents for permitting them to bring Bibles to school. Senior citizens in Balch Springs, Texas, were forbidden from saying grace before meals because the food was federally subsidised. A

San Diego pastor and his wife claim they were interrogated by a county official and warned they will face escalating fines if they continue to hold Bible studies in their home. A youth pastor was arrested in California for engaging in a casual conversation about faith in Jesus Christ in a shopping mall with two other shoppers.

An article entitled 'The Frightening Rise of Christian Persecution' on the website http://thisistheend oftheworldasweknowit.com has this comment:

> Christians in the U.S. just do not have the
> same level of freedom that they used to
> experience. For example, school teachers
> in Florida say that they are being forced to
> hide in closets to pray after a controversial
> court ruling. All expressions of Christian faith
> are being ruthlessly pushed out of the public
> sphere by very powerful interest groups. Calls
> for government repression of Christianity
> in the United States have grown louder
> than ever before. The Huffington Post even
> published a deeply disturbing article that
> calls evangelical Christianity the number one
> source of domestic terrorism in the United
> States and that calls on the Secret Service and
> the FBI to investigate and 'infiltrate' pro-life
> and evangelical Christian groups.

Not only that, but many of the hottest best selling books in recent years have publicly mocked Christianity. Just consider the titles of a few recent *New York Times* bestsellers:

God is Not Great: Why Religion Poisons Everything – by journalist Christopher Hitchens.

The End of Faith – by atheist author Sam Harris.

The God Delusion – by Richard Dawkins.

But this anti-Christian sentiment is not only held by a few elitists. The reality is that it has spread to much of the general population. For example, the following are the titles of just a few anti-Christian threads on one of the most popular political discussion forums on the Internet:

Dirty, Filthy, Christians: Treatise On The Most Dangerous Death Cult In Human History.

How can we destroy Christians?

Christians should not participate in politics.

Attention Heterosexuals! Repent! Jesus Can Finally Make You Gay!

Christians are sub-humans.

The truth is that hatred for Christians and Christianity is rapidly increasing. Jesus warned us that these days would come. In Matthew 24:9, Jesus told us how the world will treat Christians in the end times:

Then you will be handed over to be persecuted and put to death, and you will be hated by all nations because of me.

The times ahead of us are not referred to as 'the Great Tribulation' for nothing. The entire world system will be geared towards opposing the true Christian faith.

12 Assault on the Faith

One of the features of the last days in relation to the Church will be an attack on the Person of the Lord Jesus and a rejection of the Bible and its teachings. We can see this happening in many ways today. Sometimes it is a full attack on the person of Jesus Christ and sometimes a subtle infiltration of ideas which denies the faith which was delivered to us by the Apostles. One of the results of all this is to sow doubt and confusion in the minds of people and to make them reject the Christian way of salvation. All this serves the purpose of preparing the way for the antichristian world that is coming.

One of the problems I encountered when writing this chapter of the book was that this assault on the faith comes from so many quarters that to comment on each of these would entail writing a book as long or longer than this one is already. So for the sake of time and space I will point to some of the major errors which the New Testament points us to and use these to point to the pitfalls which are coming in our time. Those seeking further information on any of the areas mentioned in this chapter may find it on our website

In Luke 18:8 Jesus asks the question, '*When the Son of Man comes, will He really find faith on the earth?*' The implication of this question is 'Will He find the faith, the faith

183

which the Apostles taught?' Or will there be an apostasy, a falling away from the truth which will lead people astray?

These are some of the main areas of deception that are coming in the last days.

The Person of Jesus Christ

In 1 John 2:19-23 we read concerning the spirit of Antichrist:

> *'As you have heard that the Antichrist is coming, even now many antichrists have come, by which we know that it is the last hour. They went out from us, but they were not of us; for if they had been of us they would have continued with us; but they went out that they might be made manifest, that none of them were of us. ... Who is a liar but he who denies that Jesus is the Christ (Messiah)? He is antichrist who denies the Father and the Son. Whoever denies the Son does not have the Father either; he who acknowledges the Son has the Father also.'*

1 John 4:2-3 teaches:

> *'This is how you can recognise the Spirit of God: Every spirit that acknowledges that Jesus Christ has come in the flesh is from God, but every spirit that does not acknowledge Jesus is not from God. This is the spirit of the antichrist.'*

Here we see that John gives us two tests to recognise the spirit of Christ and the spirit of antichrist. Jesus is the Messiah with a unique relationship to the Father. In his Gospel John tells us what this relationship is when Jesus says, *'I and the Father are one'* (John 10:29). Throughout the Gospel we have repeated statements of the Lord Jesus in which He declares His divine nature. Acknowledging that Jesus Christ has come in the flesh means believing that He is God who has come to dwell in human form on the earth.

John 1:1-3 emphasises this when we read,

> *'In the beginning was the Word, and the Word was with God, and the Word was God. He was in the beginning with God. All things were made through Him, and without Him nothing was made that was made.'*

The only possible interpretation of this scripture is that the Word (Jesus) is God who was there in the beginning and through whom all things were made. This means that the universe, angels and all life forms have been created by God, but Jesus Himself has not been made, because He is God and has always existed. Just to make sure that we realize that the 'Word' is Jesus, John goes on to say,

> *'And the Word became flesh and dwelt among us, and we beheld His glory, the glory as of the only begotten of the Father, full of grace and truth.'*
>
> (John 1:14)

This means that He became flesh (a real man) and dwelt among us (lived a real life here on earth). In Philippians 2 Paul teaches that Jesus was in nature God and emptied Himself of His divine privileges (but never ceased to be God) to become man and go to the cross in order to save us. The New Testament is very clear that Jesus was not a man who became God, but God who took on human form so He could redeem lost humanity. He was fully God and fully man. All false teaching about Jesus will either deny His divinity or His humanity.

Arius

In the early Church one of the most well known denials of this truth came through Arius (256–336) who taught that Jesus is not of 'the same substance as the Father.' He said 'There was, when he was not' (i.e. Jesus was a created being). The Arian heresy, as it became known, was debated and refuted by Athanasius at the Council of Nicea (AD 325). Arius argued that Jesus is not of 'the same substance as the Father' (i.e. that he is a kind of lesser god who takes second place to the Father). Athanasius showed from the Scriptures and the witness of the early Church fathers that Jesus was not a created being and existed from eternity, being of 'one substance' with the Father.

Athanasius won the debate and the Council agreed to the following statement about the identity of Jesus in the Nicene Creed: 'I believe in one God, the Father almighty, Maker of all things visible and invisible. And in one Lord Jesus Christ, the Son of God, begotten of the Father, Light of Light, very God of very God, begotten, not made, being of one substance with the Father; by whom all things were made; who for us men, and for our salvation, came down and was incarnate and was made man; He suffered, and the third day He rose again, ascended into heaven; from thence He shall come to judge the quick and the dead.'

The Arian heresy continues to be recycled today. The most obvious example is the Jehovah's Witnesses who believe that Jesus Christ is a person distinct from God the Father. They teach that before His earthly life, Jesus was a spirit creature, Michael the archangel, who was created by God and became the 'Christ' (Messiah) at His baptism. According to Jehovah's Witnesses, Jesus is a mighty one, although not almighty as Jehovah God is. According to John 1:1 in their mistranslation of the Bible, *The New World Translation*, 'the

Word' is 'a god,' but not 'God.' They teach that Jesus 'was and is and always will be beneath Jehovah' and that 'Christ and God are not coequal'.

The Jehovah's Witnesses fit exactly into the warning given by John of those who *'went out from us, but they were not of us'* and deny that Jesus is Lord, the Word of God who became man in order to redeem us. By diminishing the status of the Lord Jesus to a created being who is a 'second in command' to Jehovah, they manifest the spirit of Antichrist of which John spoke in 1 John 2:18-23 and 1 John 4:1-3. The same applies to a multitude of cults which have arisen over the past hundred years and are increasing all the time – Mormons, Unification Church, Scientology – to name a few. There are a number of websites which give information showing why these groups do not lead to God but away from Him. http://www.christiananswers.net

This argument hit popular fiction in a big way in the hugely successful novel, 'The Da Vinci Code', which is a major attack on the foundations of Christianity. The character in the book, who is the mouthpiece for these attacks, Sir Robert Teabing, gives numerous pieces of false information. For example Teabing claims that at the Council of Nicea the Emperor Constantine led the bishops to declare Jesus as Son of God by a vote – 'a relatively close vote at that' (page 315). He says this was a new idea, because, 'Until that moment in history Jesus was viewed by His followers as a mortal prophet … a great and powerful man, but a *man* nonetheless, a mortal.'

In fact the Council of Nicea did not invent the divinity of Jesus. This was the claim of Jesus Himself, which was taught by the Apostles in the New Testament and affirmed by a huge number of writings of early Christians which predate the Council of Nicea (AD 325) by up to two hundred years. When it came to voting on this issue was it a 'relatively close vote'? Not quite. Only two out of more than 300 bishops failed to sign the creed!

Docetism

As we have seen John wrote his epistle to correct errors which were already coming into the Church and manifested themselves in so called Gnostic texts. One such error was known as Docetism, which taught that Jesus only appeared to be a man, but was really a spirit creature with no real humanity. A heretical document known as the 'Acts of John' 93 says: 'Sometimes when I went to touch him (Jesus), I met a material and solid body; and at other times when I felt him, the substance was immaterial and bodiless and as if it were not existing at all.'

In the introduction to his first epistle the real John refutes this emphasising that Jesus was really flesh and blood:

> *'That which was from the beginning, which we have heard, which we have seen with our eyes, which we have looked upon, and our hands have handled, concerning the Word of life.'*
>
> (1 John 1:1)

On the back of this false doctrine came the idea that Jesus did not really die on the cross. The 'Apocalypse of Peter' speaks of 'a substitute being put to shame'. The 'Second Treatise of the Great Seth' says that Jesus 'did not die in reality but in appearance … it was another, Simon, who bore the cross on his shoulder. I was rejoicing in the height over all. And I was laughing at their ignorance.' A similar idea appears in the Gnostic text, the Gospel of Judas, which has recently been acclaimed as a great discovery by academics.

What is remarkable is that there is a major world religion, believed by over a billion people today, which takes its cue exactly from these heretical gospels – Islam. In the Koran (Sura al-Nisaa' 4:157-158] there is a reworking of this idea that Jesus was never crucified and therefore did not rise from the dead:

'And because of their saying (in boast), 'We killed Messiah Jesus, son of Maryam (Mary), the Messenger of Allah,' **but they killed him not, nor crucified him**, but it appeared so to them the resemblance of Jesus was put over another man (and they killed that man), and those who differ therein are full of doubts. They have no (certain) knowledge, they follow nothing but conjecture. For surely, they killed him not. But Allah raised him up unto Himself (and he is in the heavens). And Allah is Ever All Powerful, All Wise.'

Islam also fulfils the other criteria of antichrist which John outlines in denying the divinity of the Lord Jesus and His oneness with the Father. The Islamic Jesus is a created being:

'The similitude of Jesus before Allah is that of Adam: he **created him from dust***, then said to him, 'Be': and he was.'*

(Koran: Sura 3.59)

The Islamic Jesus is not God in the flesh; in fact anyone who believes this will be thrown into hell:

'Surely, disbelievers are those who said. 'Allah is the third of the three (in a Trinity).' But there is no Allah (god) but One Allah. And if they cease not from what they say, verily, a painful torment will befall on the disbelievers among them.'

[al-Maa'idah 5.73]

So by applying the tests given by John we can easily see that Islam is of the spirit of antichrist. Therefore Christians and Muslims are certainly not worshipping the same God. It should also not be surprising that Islam will always oppose true Christianity and, when it has power, it will persecute Christians.

The New Age Jesus

Another assault on the true person of the Lord Jesus comes through the New Age. The idea of the New Age is tied in with the astrological view that the earth passes through the ages of the twelve zodiacs approximately every 2,000 years and we are now passing from the Age of Pisces to the Age of Aquarius. Pisces is associated with the sign of the fish and so with Christianity. Aquarius is associated with a new spirituality, which, according to some, will mean we will discover that God is within us. This view means we are now moving into a 'New Age' which will be post-Christian. Marcia Montenegro, a former astrologer who is now a Christian, describes this:

> *'Since the birth of Christ came at the beginning of the Age of Pisces, and 2,000 years have now passed, the Age of Pisces is ending and the Age of Aquarius is upon us. With the focus on the collective meanings of planetary symbols, the Age of Pisces is interpreted as a passage for all humanity that has spanned the birth of Christ until now. Christ becomes the living symbol of the Piscean Age. ... The sign of Aquarius represents recognition of one's role in collective humanity, the need for service to mankind, egalitarianism, and a desire for a*

*utopian good of the whole over the good of
the individual.'*

*The Piscean Avatar: the Jesus of Astrology by Marcia
Montenegro. www.christiananswersforthenewage.org*

This leads into the New Age view of Jesus, which is radically
different from the Jesus of the New Testament. For those
who follow the new spirituality, Jesus becomes the man who
realised Christ Consciousness, the innate divinity in all men.
In the *Metaphysical Bible Dictionary* (Unity Village, MO:
Unity, 1995), it states:

'Christ is the divine-idea of man. Each of us has within
him the Christ, just as Jesus had. The cosmic man is the
Christ. We are not persons, but factors in the cosmic mind.
Reveal yourself to yourself by affirming "I am the Christ,
son of the living God."'

In the New Age view Jesus may have been a great teacher,
a Messiah for his time, but not <u>the</u> Messiah for all time. This
idea comes out in the *Course in Miracles* written by Helen
Shuchman. She says: 'Jesus was an historical person, but the
Christ is an eternal transpersonal condition.'

What she means by this is that 'Christ' as a condition
came upon Jesus at some time in His life (usually considered
to be His baptism) and left Him when his mission ended.
That same 'Christ condition' had previously come upon
other great religious teachers of other faiths and will come
upon the New Age 'messiah' who is believed to be coming
for our time. This ties in with the real meaning of the word
'avatar', a Sanskrit word meaning 'descent' which describes
a deity coming down to earth in Hinduism. So Jesus was <u>a</u>
Messiah or Avatar for his time, but not <u>the</u> Messiah for all
time; and that now we need a new Messiah for our time.
Those who take this view, like occultist Benjamin Crème,

are looking for a new Messiah who will bring about a new world religion fusing east and west in the revelation of God being present in everyone.

By separating the historical person of Jesus from his title Christ / Messiah, the spirit of Antichrist is revealed, as we have already seen from 1 John 4:2-3.

Jesus is the unique Saviour who came once to redeem us from sin through His death on the cross and resurrection from the dead. The same Jesus is coming again, not as a 'Christ consciousness' but in the same way in which He left the earth at His ascension, in the clouds of glory, and to the same place, the Mount of Olives outside Jerusalem. On the occasion of His ascension the angel told the disciples:

> *'This same Jesus who was taken from you into heaven*
> *will so come in like manner as you saw Him go*
> *into heaven.'*

(Acts 1:11)

Yoga and alternative spirituality

Many in the West now look to the East for spiritual enlightenment and this is opening people up to yoga and transcendental meditation. The word 'yoga' derives from a Sanskrit term meaning 'to yoke' or 'to unite'. To yoke with what? The purpose of all yoga is union with ultimate reality through the realization of the divine / god-self (often called 'Self-realisation').

Yoga is now so common in our society that it has become part of the establishment, recommended in the NHS and in the education system. Yoga classes often take place in church halls and some have even developed what they call Christian yoga. In the West today 'spirituality' is more likely to be associated with doing yoga than believing in Jesus Christ as Saviour.

Yoga is often recommended as a form of 'physical fitness' while denying its connection to the Hindu religion. However according to a Hindu saying, 'There is no Hinduism without yoga and no yoga without Hinduism.' Over thousands of years Hinduism has developed numerous techniques to manipulate human consciousness in order to bring about an 'altered state of consciousness' through which you discover an inner spiritual power. These techniques are called yoga. Yoga therefore can never be seen solely as a means of gaining physical exercise, reducing stress or as a medical therapy.

In Hatha yoga body postures (asanas) are intended to immobilise the whole body. Practising them will enable the body to become completely motionless and hardened in fixed positions. Meditation words (mantras) serve to immobilise the consciousness. Mantras are usually the names of gods used for worship. Symbolic body movements in yoga are designed to close 'all nine doors of the body', so that no sense perception from the outside penetrates into the mind. When all outer sensation is shut off the body itself will create sense perceptions of an inner kind, with an inner light and an inner pleasure.

I once talked to a yoga teacher who became a Christian. He said that he did not teach his pupils anything about Hinduism to begin with, but simply taught them the techniques of yoga. They then experienced things that they could not explain and he interpreted their experiences in such a way that would lead them deeper into the Hindu philosophy of discovering God within yourself. As such it is clearly connected to the occult as New Age devotee Miriam Starhawk made clear in an article in *Yoga Journal* (May 1986):

'The longing for expanded consciousness has taken many of us on a spiritual journey to the East and to Hindu, Taoist and Buddhist

concepts. Eastern religions offer a radically different approach to spirituality than Judeo-Christian traditions. Their goal is not to know God but to be God. In many ways these philosophies are close to witchcraft.'

(Yoga Journal, May 1986)

The idea that we can be 'as God' goes right back to the opening pages of the Bible where it is seen as the deception of the Devil, not the source of enlightenment. This idea has become very popular in the West. M. Scott Peck, a psychologist whose books are popular even in some Christian bookstores, writes,

'God wants us to become himself (or herself or itself). We are growing toward godhood. God is the goal of evolution.'

(The Road Less Travelled)

Maharishi Mahesh Yogi says, 'Man is divine; the inner man is fully divine. Be still and know you are God. When you know you are God you will begin to live Godhood.'

Swami Muktananda brought the tradition of Siddha Yoga to the West, giving initiation to thousands of spiritual seekers. His teaching is, 'Kneel to your own self. Honour and worship your own being. God dwells within you as You.'

On the other hand, the Apostle Paul wrote,

'I know that in me, that is in my flesh, dwells no good thing.'

(Romans 7:18)

We do not discover God within ourselves, although there is no doubt that Satan does give counterfeit spiritual experiences of light and peace which convince people that they have encountered God. We come to know God by being born again of the Holy Spirit as we repent of our sins and believe in the Lord Jesus who came from heaven to earth in order to save us and give us eternal life. Jesus said:

'Behold I stand at the door and knock. If anyone hears My voice and opens the door I will come into him and dine with him and he with Me.'

(Revelation 3:20)

Attack upon the uniqueness of Christ

'"And if I go and prepare a place for you, I will come again and receive you to Myself; that where I am, there you may be also. And where I go you know, and the way you know." Thomas said to Him, "Lord, we do not know where You are going, and how can we know the way?" Jesus said to him, "I am the way, the truth, and the life. No one comes to the Father except through Me."'

(John 14:6)

It is interesting that it is in the context of speaking of His return that Jesus makes this statement that He is the only way to the Father. Today, as we get nearer to the day of His return, this statement is under attack as never before. The most politically incorrect statement you can make in public life today is to say that Jesus is the one way to God. If you go on to make the obvious deduction from this that other faiths, no matter how sincere their devotees may be, do not lead to God, you can be sure to have howls of condemnation fall down on your head.

The multi faith view that all religions lead to God has become virtually the official religion of Britain today. If you make any statement denying this you can guarantee to be frozen out of having a platform in the media or in the educational system. Leaders of churches, when interviewed on the media, will almost always make some compromising statement on this subject and leave people with the idea that Christians accept that all roads lead to God. This idea is said to be vital to the harmony and unity of society.

A report by Carl Teichrib (www.forcingchange.org), who attended the World Religions Summit in Winnipeg Canada, which took place in June 2010, made interesting reading on this subject. Carl, who is an evangelical Christian, noted that:

◊ The only time the name 'Jesus Christ' came up was when He was compared with Buddha and Mohammad as a religious figure. Nobody dared present Him as 'the way, the truth and the life... the only way to the Father.' (John 14:6).

◊ Participants apologised for two millennia of Christian evangelism which has proclaimed that Jesus Christ is Lord and Saviour of all and sought 'to make the whole world Christian'.

The basic message of the conference was: 'Religions need to unify if the planet is to survive.'

The idea of unifying religions in order to save the world has long been on the agenda of a number of bodies, some of which are linked to the UN. Dr Robert Muller, former Assistant Secretary General of the United Nations, said, 'My great personal dream is to forge a tremendous alliance between all religions and spiritual groups, and the UN. We desperately need a United Religions Organisation to bring reconciliation, unity and peace to all the peoples of our world.'

On this subject there has been an approach by Muslims to the Pope. 138 scholars from every sect of Islam have signed a letter to the Pope and other leaders of Christian denominations warning that the 'survival of the world' is at stake if Muslims and Christians do not make peace with each other. 'Finding common ground between Muslims and Christians is not simply a matter for polite ecumenical dialogue between selected religious leaders,' the Muslim scholars say, noting that Christians and Muslims make up over a third and a fifth of humanity respectively. 'If Muslims and Christians are not at peace, the world cannot be at peace.'

Such a movement flies in the face of the Gospel message that Jesus is the Saviour of the world, the one mediator between God and humanity. For Christians this would mean joining the God who created us and redeemed us in the Lord Jesus Christ with all other gods. The Bible declares these to be idols which cannot save us (Psalm 96:5, Isaiah 45:18-23). Salvation comes through faith in Jesus Christ alone, because He alone has paid the price of sin through His death and resurrection from the dead.

This movement opposes Bible-believing Christians who seek to spread the Gospel, and may well end up working for the banning of open evangelism by Christians. It ties in with the picture of the woman riding the beast (false religion in alliance with the political power) which we have in Revelation 17.

Most of the participants in such conferences are liberal Christians who deny the Gospel message anyway. However there are signs of this way of thinking trickling down into evangelical churches. Roger Oakland attended 'The Rethink Conference' and gave this comment on what he saw there:

'For nearly two thousand years, most professing Christians have seen the Bible as the foundation for the Christian faith.

The overall view at the Rethink Conference, however, is that Christianity, as we have known it, has run its course and must be replaced…. Speakers insisted that Christianity must be re-thought and re-invented if the name of Jesus Christ is going to survive here on planet earth.'

Brian McLaren has said, "You see if we have a new world, we will need a new church." The idea is that in order to reach the so-called postmodern world we need to revise and update Christianity. He says that this will involve a "new set of answers, a different way of being Christians."

One of the ideas for re-thinking Christianity is that instead of a programme of preaching the Gospel to the world, Christians should join a peace plan to save the world. One of the biggest influences in this direction has been Rick Warren and his Global P.E.A.C.E. Plan which has 500,000 churches in 162 nations as part of his network. The P.E.A.C.E. plan identifies the 'giants' of humanity's ills as spiritual emptiness, self-centred leadership, poverty, disease, and illiteracy, which he hopes to eradicate by (P)lanting churches, (E)quipping leaders, (A)ssisting the poor, (C)aring for the sick, and (E)ducating the next generation.

Rick Warren reasons that since there are 2.3 billion Christians worldwide, they could potentially form a vast 'army of compassion' of 'people of faith' such as the world has not yet experienced. Although I question the figure of there being 2.3 billion Christians in the world, I have no problem with the idea that an 'army of compassion' should be mobilised in order to help those in need. Clearly this is a good goal. It could be seen to fit in with Jesus' goal of world evangelism, as long as it includes the supreme human need of accepting salvation through faith in Jesus Christ alone.

However in the process of putting this plan into action, the need for non-Christians to be saved through faith in Jesus is being downplayed. This becomes much less important than meeting people's social needs. It also ends up with another version of the inter faith idea that all faiths are equally valid. In order to put the plan into action you have to find 'the man of peace' who could be of any faith who will work with you to attack the 'five giants.'

Rick Warren serves on the advisory council of Tony Blair's Faith Foundation, which is avowedly inter-faith in its programme. Blair has said, "I'll dedicate the rest of my life to uniting the world's religions. Faith is part of our future, and faith and the values it brings with it are an essential part of making globalisation work."

Rick Warren appeared at a meeting presided over by Tony Blair of the Davos 2008 World Economic Forum (a gathering of leading world industrialists, politicians and media people) to present his programme. At this conference he declared, "The future of the world is not secularism, but religious pluralism. … We cannot solve these problems without involving people of faith and their religious institutions. It isn't going to happen any other way. On this planet there are about 20 million Jews, there are about 600 million Buddhists, there are about 800 million Hindus, there are over 1 billion Muslims, and there are 2.3 billion Christians. If you take people of faith out of the equation, you have ruled out five-sixths of the world. And if we only leave it up to secular people to solve these major problems, it isn't going to happen."

One of the panellists at this gathering then said that religious leaders of different faiths must not seek to deny the 'authenticity' of other people's faith, or suggest that they are 'illegitimate, or consigned to some kind of evil end.' What he meant was that Christians should not say that Jesus is the only Saviour and that those who die without saving faith in Jesus Christ are eternally lost. Neither Rick Warren nor any Christian present defended the Christian position that Jesus is the only Saviour and without Him we are lost. This is the cost of participating in inter faith gatherings aiming to save the world through religious pluralism.

It is a cost that Emerging Church leader Brian McLaren seems willing to pay. He has said that the future way of life for the Christian will 'require us to join humbly and charitably with people of other faiths – Muslim, Hindu, Buddhist, Jewish, secularists, and others – in pursuit of peace, environmental stewardship, and justice for all people, things that matter greatly to the heart of God.' (July 28, 2008, on *ChristianPost.com)*. However the Gospel shows us that the most important thing to the heart of God is *'that all should come to repentance'* and believe the Gospel.

The Bible as the Word of God

It is interesting that when debating with Christians, Muslims often support their case by referring to liberal Christian clergy who have made statements denying the divinity of Jesus. Here we come to another manifestation of the spirit of antichrist which is very much inside the professing Church today – liberal theology / modernism which denies the most basic teachings of the New Testament.

In his letter to Timothy Paul states his faith in the verbal inspiration of Scripture by God:

> *'All Scripture is given by inspiration of God, and is profitable for doctrine, for reproof, for correction, for instruction in righteousness, that the man of God may be complete, thoroughly equipped for every good work.'*
> (2 Timothy 3:16-17)

Paul goes on to warn of the coming time when people will turn aside from the truth of this message to believing myths and fables.

'For the time will come when they will not endure sound doctrine, but according to their own desires, because they have itching ears, they will heap up for themselves teachers; and they will turn their ears away from the truth, and be turned aside to fables.'

(2 Timothy 4:3-4)

That time has certainly come. One of the major problems we face in trying to tell people about Jesus today is the widespread perception that the Gospels themselves are mythical, unreliable documents written long after the event. The main source of this comes from the Church itself and liberal theological colleges teaching Higher Critical Theology. This theology denies that the Bible is the Word of God, and questions the basic teaching of the Bible: the Creation account, the miraculous interventions of God in the Old Testament, the Virgin Birth, Jesus' miracles, His sinless life, His death as an atoning sacrifice for the sins of the world, His resurrection and the promise of His return in power and glory to judge the world in righteousness. In other words, it means abandoning the Bible as the Word of God. If you accept all this, there is no point in going to church and believing in Jesus.

I have been working on a reply to a book written by Asher Norman, an Orthodox Jew, called '26 Reasons why Jews don't believe in Jesus.' One of his reasons for this is his claim: 'The Epistles and the Gospels were not written by actual witnesses to the events they described.' He goes on to say that the Gospels were written by unknown men who took the names of Matthew, Mark, Luke and John up to 150 years after the events they describe.

On the basis of Higher Critical Theology Asher Norman says that the Epistles were written in the first century with no mention of the Gospel accounts. He says that the Gospels were not written at the time the Epistles were written and that the authors of the Epistles really knew nothing about Jesus as described in the Gospels. He goes on to say that Mark was written in around 125 CE and Matthew, Luke and John around 175 CE.

In this he is joined by a host of different sources today which undermine faith in the Bible, many of them coming from within the Church. What is most significant is that while the assault on the Bible is unceasing and comes from a multitude of sources, virtually no one bothers to bring the same kind of criticism to the Koran or the Gita or other sacred texts.

In addition to Higher Critical Theology the world is cashing in on the clergy's unbelief and bringing the most vicious attacks on the Word of God which are propagated in books, films and on the Internet. These attacks are believed by millions who are thereby infected with the spirit of Antichrist.

The Da Vinci Code claims that the 'Bible as we know it today was collated by the pagan Roman Emperor Constantine the Great ... More than eighty gospels were considered for the New Testament, and yet only a relative few were chosen for inclusion – Matthew, Mark, Luke and John among them' (page 313). He claims this decision was taken at the Council of Nicea. This is completely inaccurate because the Council of Nicea said nothing about which books should be included in the New Testament.

In his book *Evidence that Demands a Verdict,* Josh McDowell shows how the writings of early Christians show a clear acceptance of the four Gospels as the genuine account of the life and ministry of the Lord Jesus. Irenaeus, Bishop of Lyons around AD 180, wrote:

> *'For as there are four quarters of the world in which we live and four universal winds, and as the Church is dispersed over all the earth, and the gospel is the pillar and the*

base of the Church and the breath of life, so
*it is natural that it should have **four pillars**,*
breathing immortality from every quarter
and kindling the life of men anew. Whence it
is manifest that the Word ... has given us the
*gospel in **fourfold form**, but held together by*
one Spirit.'

(Against Heresies III)

He goes on to affirm the Gospels written by Matthew, Mark, Luke and John as the authentic accounts. (*Evidence* page 63-4). The 'eighty gospels', which the Da Vinci Code claims were considered for inclusion in the New Testament, were never in fact considered as for the most part they were made up of later heretical documents which were rejected by the early Church.

There is an enormous amount of manuscript evidence for the New Testament, as we know it today, way beyond any other ancient document, including the Old Testament. There are more than 5,300 known Greek manuscripts of the New Testament. Add over 10,000 Latin Vulgate and at least 9,300 other early versions and we have more than 24,000 manuscript copies of portions of the New Testament in existence today. No other document of antiquity even begins to approach such numbers and attestation. The world's second best documented ancient book is Homer's Iliad of which we have 643 manuscripts.

Quotations from the New Testament in early Christian writings are so extensive that it could virtually be reconstructed from these writings without the use of New Testament manuscripts. There are no less than 36,289 quotations from the New Testament in the works of the early Christian writers Justin Martyr, Irenaeus, Clement of Alexandria, Origen, Tertullian, Hippolytus and Eusebius.

(Information from 'Evidence that demands a verdict' by Josh McDowell).

The New Testament itself gives us some very good clues as to when it was written. If we take as a starting point the Book of Acts we have some events recorded there which can be checked against Roman history and the writings of Josephus. In chapters 24-25 Paul is taken before the Roman governors, Felix and Festus. We know from Josephus that Festus succeeded Felix in 59 AD and died in 62 AD. According to Acts 27 Festus granted Paul's request to be tried in Rome. After surviving a storm at sea on the way, Paul arrived in Rome and stayed there for two years (Acts 28:30). This would take us up to around 62AD. Acts ends quite abruptly without mentioning the fact that Paul was executed in Rome probably around 65 AD. Luke does mention the death of James, the brother of John, in chapter 12. James plays a very minor part in the Book of Acts, so why does Luke not mention the death of Paul who is the main subject of the entire section from Acts 13-28? The most obvious answer is that he completed Acts before Paul was executed.

So the most likely date for writing Acts is around 62-65 AD. In the opening verses of Acts Luke describes his former book in which he wrote about all that Jesus began to do and teach (i.e. the Gospel of Luke). So the Gospel of Luke must have been written before this. In the opening verses of his Gospel, Luke writes of those who had previously undertaken to write an account of the things 'that have been fulfilled among us' (i.e. the life of Jesus). The logical assumption from this is that the Gospels of Matthew and Mark were written before Luke.

Regarding the rest of the New Testament Paul's letters must have been written before he died! 2 Peter 3:15 contains reference to Paul as to someone still alive, so Peter's letters were written before Paul died. Jude contains material very similar to 2 Peter so was probably written at about the same time. Hebrews must have been written before the destruction of the Temple, whatever one's view about whether or not it was written by Paul. James was written probably by James the bishop of the Jerusalem church who, according to Josephus, was put to death in 62 AD. That has covered the entire New Testament apart from John's writings.

John was the longest living of the Apostles, exiled to Patmos under the persecutions of Emperor Domitian (81-96 AD), so his books could have been written later, and certainly the early Church tradition is that John wrote his Gospel after the Synoptic Gospels. Liberal theologian John Robinson in his book 'Redating the New Testament' came to the conclusion that John's Gospel was written before the destruction of the Temple. John 21:19 possibly implies that Peter was still alive at the time of writing John's Gospel.

By this method we have placed most of the New Testament being written before 70 AD.

Rejection of Creation and Judgement

Peter wrote in his epistle that:

> 'Scoffers will come in the last days, walking according to their own lusts, and saying, 'Where is the promise of His coming? For since the fathers fell asleep, all things continue as they were from the beginning of creation.'
> For this they wilfully forget: that by the word of God the heavens were of old, and the earth standing out of water and in the water, by which the world that then existed perished, being flooded with water. But the heavens and the earth which are now preserved by the same word, are reserved for fire until the day of judgment and perdition of ungodly men.'   (2 Peter 3:3-7)

If you analyse what Peter has written here he is saying that in the last days people will scoff at the following:

◊   The promise of the Second Coming of Christ.

◊   The idea of a special creation by the Word of God.

◊   The historic event of the Flood.

This means a rejection of what the Bible says about the beginning and the end of our world.

The beginning

Obviously the main attack on the beginning part comes via evolution. Today it is almost required thinking to accept evolution as a proven scientific fact. Richard Dawkins has said that anyone who disbelieves evolution is either 'ignorant, stupid or insane.' Most people do not want to be considered any of these so they go along with evolutionary teaching. Sadly much of the professing Church also accepts evolution, missing the point that if it is true, then not only is Genesis a myth, but there are serious problems with the rest of the Bible. Creation is taught throughout the Bible from Genesis to Revelation and is assumed to be true by the Lord Jesus and the Apostles.

The Bible teaches that in the beginning God created the heavens and the earth. He created all creatures with the ability to reproduce *'after their own kind'* and created humans in His image (i.e. with a different nature to animals and capable of a spiritual relationship with God). Because of human disobedience to God the relationship between God and humanity was lost and sin and death entered the world. This event, known as the Fall, has affected not just human beings but the whole of creation. God promised a redeemer who would save us from the consequences of sin and death

– the *'seed of the woman'* who would bruise the head of the serpent (Genesis 3:15), the earliest prophecy of the Messiah in the Bible.

The Fall was followed by the catastrophe of the Flood which was worldwide and has further altered conditions on earth. According to the biblical view of 'catastrophism' (the present world being shaped by the catastrophes of the Fall and the Flood), the world is relatively young. There are a number of evidences of the Flood as a relatively recent historical event which shaped our world as it is today. Jesus said there would be a further catastrophe (*'as in the days of Noah'*) at the end of this age, which would precede His Second Coming and the millennial kingdom age in which He would reign over a renewed earth.

Evolution teaches that there were millions of years of death and destruction before humans appeared on the scene, so there is no connection between sin and death and therefore no need for Jesus to die as a sacrifice for the sins of the world. Opponents of Christianity understand this. Dave Hunt quotes *The American Atheist* in his book *Occult Invasion* (p.35):

'But if death preceded man and was not a result of Adams's sin, then sin is a fiction. If sin is a fiction we have no need for a Saviour. Evolution destroys utterly and finally the very reason for Jesus' earthly life. If Jesus was not the Redeemer who died for our sins, and this is what evolution means, then Christianity is nothing.'

Evolutionists like to point out that the Pope and the Archbishop of Canterbury both accept evolution, as do liberal evangelicals and almost all of our Bible colleges. However, as Ken Ham has pointed out, if we reject the Genesis account of creation, we destroy the foundation on which the whole of God's revelation is built and the house comes tumbling down in the end.

There are a number of scientific issues raising doubts about evolution which are beyond the scope of this book to go into in depth. What existed before the Big Bang? How did an explosion of either nothing, or a super dense ball, cause an ordered universe to come into being? How did life emerge out of non-life? Every cell contains millions of pieces of information vital for life to come into being and to continue, so where did that information come from? How could creatures have evolved vital organs (sight, heart, brain, ability to reproduce etc) over millions of generations, when those organs were necessary for the survival of just one generation?

I do not have space here to give more scientific arguments for Creation but recommend the work of *Answers in Genesis* and *Creation Ministries International* for this. *The Answers Book* has a number of good arguments for the Genesis account being true. Other books on the subject are:

> *The Lie – Evolution* by Ken Ham. This book shows the consequences of rejecting the Genesis account and why evolution is based on false assumptions.
>
> *In Six Days*. This book answers the question 'Can any scientist with a PhD believe the idea of a literal six day creation?' 50 scientists from around the world say 'Yes.' This book is for the more technically minded!

Extensive websites on topics relating to creation and evolution written by scientists can be found at www.answersingenesis. org, www.c-r-t.co.uk and www.creation.com.

The End

The passage in Peter also implies that there will be a rejection of the idea of the Second Coming of Christ in the last days. We see this happening now, especially among professing

Christians. The Lord's return has become almost a taboo subject in many churches. When I speak about the Second Coming at meetings around the country the most common comment I hear is 'Why don't we hear about this subject in our churches?' There are a number of reasons for this.

Most Bible colleges are a-millennial in their theology. A-millennial means there is no millennium. In other words the second coming of Christ is followed by no millennium (or 1000 year reign of Christ) and it is the end of the world. This conflicts with the pre-millennial view of Scripture which teaches that this age will end with a time of unique trouble following which Christ will return and reign on the earth during the Millennium (for 1000 years). Pre-millennial theology is largely neglected or even ridiculed in many Bible colleges, therefore most pastors who end up leading churches have been taught to reject it. Nevertheless a literal interpretation of Scripture must mean that Jesus the Messiah returns before (pre) the Millennium which is a 1000 year reign of the Messiah from Jerusalem during which time there is peace and justice on earth (Isaiah 2:1-4, 11-12, Zechariah 14, Revelation 20).

A large section of the charismatic movement has accepted 'post-millennial' teaching. This means that the Messiah will come back after (post) the millennium. In other words the Church will win the world for Jesus by means of a great revival with signs and wonders and so bring in Christian world rule. Preachers have prophesied that they will see whole cities and nations won for Jesus as extraordinary miracles take place and people turn to Him in huge numbers and fill the churches (or even the football stadiums). They say that the pre-millennial view that this age ends in a time of tribulation is 'defeatist' and 'negative' and we should expect the global triumph of the Church through claiming the ground for Jesus and demonstrating His power through signs and wonders. 'Prophecies' of imminent Christian revival come and go with regularity. We generally find that Christian influence in our society has become weaker, while Islam, New Age and paganism get stronger. The prophecies of the Bible speak of a time of tribulation in the last days of this age, not of the Christianisation of the world (Matthew 24, Revelation 6-19).

One of the key signs of the last days is the return of the Jewish people to Israel. Because of the conflicts in Israel, the problems of the Palestinians and some hostility to Jewish people, Israel has become unpopular in the world. Many churches, especially in the UK, are now siding with the Palestinians against Israel and deny that there is any biblical significance in the restoration of Israel. We also find that most of the Church today believes 'replacement theology' – that the Church has replaced Israel and so prophecies about the return of the Jewish people to Israel apply to the Church.

It has also been said that teaching on the end times is dangerous and divisive. Bishop Mark Hanson of the Evangelical Lutheran Church of America has called for 'Catholics, Eastern Orthodox, Anglican and Lutheran churches to come together to combat a fundamentalist reading of Scripture' and create a 'ministry of reconciliation,' that will 'result of Christ breaking down the dividing walls reconciling the whole creation to God's self.' Hanson says that those who take the Bible literally and believe that we are living in the end times are holding back the cause of Christ, which he suggests is to unite all of creation and produce a planetary utopia. From 'Evangelicals and Catholics Together and the Rejection of End-Time Christians' by Roger Oakland.

On the other hand, Sir Isaac Newton, the famous scientist who lived from 1643 – 1727, was a Bible-believing Christian.

He wrote: 'About the time of the end, a body of men will be raised up who will turn their attention to the Prophecies and insist upon their literal interpretation in the midst of much clamour and opposition.'

The Lord who bought us

In 2 Peter 2 we read:

> *'But there were also false prophets among the people, even as there will be false teachers among you, who will secretly bring in destructive heresies, even denying the Lord who bought them, and bring on themselves swift destruction. And many will follow their destructive ways, because of whom the way of truth will be blasphemed. By covetousness they will exploit you with deceptive words; for a long time their judgment has not been idle, and their destruction does not slumber.'*

Peter warns that people would *'deny the Lord who bought them'* – in other words deny the central message of our faith that the Lord Jesus redeemed us through his once-and-for-all sacrifice at Calvary. The most dangerous deniers of this in the last days will be professing ministers of the Christian faith.

One of the most obvious examples of this is the Roman Catholic doctrine of the Mass. The Catholic belief is that the wafer taken at communion becomes the body of Christ (transubstantiation). This means that Jesus needs to be sacrificed continually through the Mass as the priest changes the bread and the wine are literally into his body and blood. Article 267 of the Catechism says –

> *'The bread and the wine are changed into the Body and Blood of Christ by the power of God, to whom nothing is impossible or difficult.'*

Article 278 says –

> *'The Holy Mass is one and the same Sacrifice*
> *with that of the Cross, inasmuch as Christ*
> *who offered himself, a bleeding victim on the*
> *Cross to his heavenly Father, continues to*
> *offer himself in an unbloody manner on the*
> *altar through the ministry of his priests.'*

But the Bible teaches that Christ's sacrifice was complete and final and can never be repeated. Communion or the Lord's Supper is the remembrance of that sacrifice. On the cross Jesus said *'It is finished'* and then *'gave up his spirit'* (John 20:30). By this He meant the work of redemption was finished and there was no further offering that needs to be made. In Hebrews 9:28 we read, *'And as it is appointed for men to die once, but after this the judgment, so Christ was offered once to bear the sins of many.'* Saying that He was offered **once** means that He cannot be offered over and over again through the Mass.

In Roman Catholicism traditions and the uninspired books of the Apocrypha are believed to be as much the Word of God as the Bible itself. Vatican II states that –

'The task of authentically interpreting the word of God whether written or handed on (i.e. the Tradition) has been entrusted **exclusively** to the living, teaching office of the church.'

This means that only the Catholic Church can interpret the Bible properly and infallibly. In reality, the Catholic Church throughout history has misinterpreted the Bible, adding things that are not there and leaving out things that are there. As a result it is left with a false Jesus.

Catholicism has elevated Mary to a position which has no basis at all in the New Testament. She is called 'mother of God' (Catechism, Article 167) and 'Queen of Heaven'

(Article 168a). Article 117 says: 'All mankind has contracted the guilt and stain of original sin, except The Blessed Virgin and her Divine Son.' There is now a campaign to have Mary officially proclaimed a Mediatrix (co mediator with Jesus between God and humanity). Catholics address prayers to Mary as a mediator already in the 'Hail Mary' prayer. *'Hail Mary, Mother of God, pray for us sinners, now and at the hour of our death. Amen.'*

In the New Testament Mary was the earthly mother of the Lord Jesus and was faithful in the task God gave her to do. But she was by no means the 'mother of God'. She was neither 'immaculately' conceived, nor assumed into heaven, but she was saved, as you and I may be, through her faith. She cannot pray for us sinners. Only Jesus can do that. In her prayer, recorded in Luke 2, she says, *'My spirit has rejoiced in God my Saviour.'* (Luke 2:47). She conceived supernaturally by the Holy Spirit to bring forth Jesus by Virgin Birth. However after the birth of her 'firstborn son' she had other children in the normal way with Joseph as the father. In fact Matthew 13:55-56 implies that she had at least six other children after Jesus was born.

The elevation of Mary to the role given her by the Roman Catholic Church shows a connection to the Babylonian mystery cults. These had a goddess mother figure, known as the Queen of Heaven. We now have apparitions of 'Mary' appearing to Catholics around the world, claiming that the Rosary and the Immaculate Heart of Mary are going to save the world. The messages given are a deception which will not lead people to a place of safety or prevent the 'approaching holocaust' because the peace of the world has not been entrusted to Mary but to the Lord Jesus Christ.

Apparently neither the mediation of Jesus nor Mary is sufficient for Catholicism, because even devout Catholics have to suffer for a time in purgatory, 'a place where souls suffer for a time after death on account of their sins'

(*Catechism*, Article 106). But the real Jesus was able to say to the thief on the cross,

'Today you will be with Me in Paradise.'

(Luke 23:43)

This man was saved by his faith in Jesus and, although he had no doubt committed many sins, he did not have to spend any time in purgatory, a place which is never mentioned once in the Bible.

Despite the many errors of Rome, today we are finding that more and more supposedly evangelical Christians are saying that the Roman Catholic Church is an authentic Church which is working for the evangelisation of the world.

I was sent a leaflet announcing 'We are one!' inviting participation in 'Manchester's Walk of Christian Witness' from Salford Roman Catholic Cathedral to Manchester (Anglican) Cathedral. Taking part were 'Christians from across the nationalities and traditions' from Catholic to Pentecostal and the aim was 'to pray and praise as one and be seen as one.' Another meeting announces that 'God has made a way to heal our wounded, hurting society. ... His purposes are fulfilled when Christians of all traditions come together as the ONE Body of Christ.'

But are we all one? If we believe the Gospel and the teaching of the Apostles in the New Testament, we are not one with Rome or with liberal churches.

The many errors of the Roman Catholic Church take away from the true message of salvation through repentance and faith in the sacrifice of the Lord Jesus on the cross. Despite this many supposed evangelical leaders today are making statements which show they believe Roman Catholicism to be a valid expression of the Christian faith.

This is another sign of the apostasy that will come in the last days of this age.

Protestant denials of the Lord who bought us

It is not just Roman Catholicism which has a problem in this area. In November 1993, the World Council of Churches sponsored a Re-imaging conference in Minneapolis, Minnesota. Some 2,000 women 'seeking to change Christianity' attended. Speaking at this conference, Virginia Mollenkott, who served as a stylistic consultant for the New International Version of the Bible, said:

> *'Jesus is our elder brother, the trailblazer and constant companion for us – ultimately he is among many brothers and sisters in an eternal, equally worthy sibling-hood. First born only in the sense that he was the first to show us that it is possible to live in oneness with the divine source while we are here on this planet. As an incest survivor, I can no longer worship in a theological context that depicts God as an abusive parent (referring to Christ's death on the cross) and Jesus as the obedient, trusting child.'*

Referring to Christ's death on the cross as depicting God as 'an abusive parent' is blasphemous, and something which evangelical Christians should decisively reject.

Brian McLaren, a leader of the Emerging Church, referred to the teaching that Jesus took the sins of the world on himself as something that 'sounds like divine child abuse' in his book, *The Story We Find Ourselves In*. Later in this book he says that Jesus did not know why He had to die.

A basic reading of the Gospels shows that this is not the case. Jesus said,

> *'The Son of Man did not come to be served, but to serve, and to give His life a ransom for many.'*
>> (Matthew 20:28; see also Matthew 16:21, Luke 22:20, Luke 24:44-47, and John 12:31-32)

The Apostles also had no doubt as to why Jesus died. Peter wrote:

> *'For Christ also suffered once for sins, the just for the unjust, that He might bring us to God, being put to death in the flesh but made alive by the Spirit.'*
>> (1 Peter 3:18; see also 1 Corinthians 15:3-4)

When John wanted to explain his statement '*God is love*' he went on to write:

> *'In this is love, not that we loved God, but that He loved us and sent His Son to be the propitiation for our sins.'*
>> (1 John 4:10)

Propitiation carries the idea of appeasing the wrath of an offended person and being reconciled to him. It is the unique work of Jesus Christ on the cross, by which He takes the wrath of God against sin upon Himself. So He enables us to be reconciled to God by taking the punishment that we deserve in order that we can be pardoned. Otherwise we have to pay the penalty for our sin ourselves.

This is the central message of the Christian faith: that the Lord Jesus, who knew no sin, died as an atoning sacrifice for the sins of the world, so that we who are sinners could be redeemed through His blood. Take that message away and there is no message of salvation left in Christianity. What will remain is an apostate Church which will go into the Tribulation period and join in the Babylon world religious system prophesied in Revelation 17.

Conclusion

In the Letter of Jude we read:

> *'Beloved, while I was very diligent to write to you concerning our common salvation, I found it necessary to write to you exhorting you to contend earnestly for the faith which was once for all delivered to the saints. For certain men have crept in unnoticed, who long ago were marked out for this condemnation, ungodly men, who turn the grace of our God into lewdness and deny the only Lord God and our Lord Jesus Christ.'*
>
> (Jude 3-4)

A number of scriptures imply that in the last days before Jesus returns there will be a great departure from the truth and even a *'famine of hearing the word of God'* (Amos 8:11). Speaking of the signs of the end of the age, Jesus warned of spiritual deception first of all:

> *'Take heed that no one deceive you, for many will come in my name saying, "I am the Christ (Messiah)" and will deceive many.'*
>
> (Matthew 24:4-5)

13 So What Will Happen to the Church?

Most of the official denominations of Christianity will become more and more apostate and deny the fundamentals of the faith. Liberal theology and ecumenism will undermine the authority of the Bible and a number of teachings will come in which contradict the 'apostles' doctrine'. The nearer we get to the end, the more true Christians will face persecution and opposition to their faith. Many will find it hard to find a church where the Word of God is regularly preached. Open evangelism will be more and more restricted in nations around the world, including the western nations, as 'political correctness' makes it difficult to say anything which goes against the flow of the opinions propagated and allowed by those in power.

The true Church of Jesus Christ will be known to God and will make Him known throughout the world despite much opposition:

> *'Nevertheless the solid foundation of God stands, having*
> *this seal: "The Lord knows those who are His," and,*
> *"Let everyone who names the name of Christ depart*
> *from iniquity."'*

> (2 Timothy 2:19)

'And Jesus came and spoke to them, saying, "All
authority has been given to Me in heaven and on earth.
Go therefore and make disciples of all the nations,
baptizing them in the name of the Father and of the
Son and of the Holy Spirit, teaching them to observe all
things that I have commanded you; and lo, I am with you
always, even to the end of the age."'

(Matthew 28:18-20)

Despite all the negative signs around us we see that the message of the Gospel is going out to all the nations, and that there are believers in Jesus from every nation. This does not mean that the nations will be 'christianised,' because the true Church will be a minority saved by grace amidst a majority who are in rebellion against God, as we see from the following verses:

'Enter by the narrow gate; for wide is the gate and broad
is the way that leads to destruction, and there are many
who go in by it. Because narrow is the gate and difficult
is the way which leads to life, and there are few who
find it.'

(Matthew 7:13-14)

'Even so then, at this present time there is a remnant
according to the election of grace.'

(Romans 11:5)

The true Church will be saved from the wrath to come by the blood of Jesus and be caught up to meet Him as He comes in the air:

'For this we say to you by the word of the Lord, that we
who are alive and remain until the coming of the Lord

will by no means precede those who are asleep. For the Lord Himself will descend from heaven with a shout, with the voice of an archangel, and with the trumpet of God. And the dead in Christ will rise first. Then we who are alive and remain shall be caught up together with them in the clouds to meet the Lord in the air. And thus we shall always be with the Lord. Therefore comfort one another with these words.'

(1 Thessalonians 4:15-18)

'And they sang a new song, saying: "You are worthy to take the scroll, And to open its seals; For You were slain, And have redeemed us to God by Your blood out of every tribe and tongue and people and nation."'

(Revelation 5:9)

As well as the true Church, there is also an apostate Church. The apostate Church will go into the Tribulation period. This Church denies the blood of Jesus as the only means whereby sins are forgiven and is willing to make a compromise with other faiths in an interfaith union. This interfaith union will be known as Babylon the Great, a false religious system, which will cooperate with the coming Antichrist during the first half of the Tribulation. He will use this religious system to gain power.

'Then one of the seven angels who had the seven bowls came and talked with me, saying to me: "Come, I will show you the judgment of the great harlot who sits on many waters, with whom the kings of the earth committed fornication, and the inhabitants of the earth were made drunk with the wine of her fornication." So he carried me away in the Spirit into the wilderness. And I saw a woman

*sitting on a scarlet beast, which was full of names
of blasphemy, having seven heads and ten horns.
The woman was arrayed in purple and scarlet, and
adorned with gold and precious stones and pearls,
having in her hand a golden cup full of abominations
and the filthiness of her fornication. And on her
forehead a name was written: MYSTERY, BABYLON
THE GREAT, THE MOTHER OF HARLOTS AND OF
THE ABOMINATIONS OF THE EARTH. I saw the
woman, drunk with the blood of the saints and with
the blood of the martyrs of Jesus. And when I saw
her, I marvelled with great amazement.'*

(Revelation 17:1-6)

This religious system is a whore (unfaithful) as opposed to
the faithful wife of Christ described in Revelation 19:7-9:

*'Let us be glad and rejoice and give Him glory, for the
marriage of the Lamb has come, and His wife has made
herself ready. And to her it was granted to be arrayed
in fine linen, clean and bright, for the fine linen is the
righteous acts of the saints. Then he said to me, "Write:
'Blessed are those who are called to the marriage supper
of the Lamb!' " And he said to me, "These are the true
sayings of God."'*

Following the Rapture of the Church, 144,000 Jewish people
will supernaturally receive the revelation that Yeshua, Jesus,
is the promised Messiah and go out with great power to
preach the Gospel in the first half of the Great Tribulation
(Revelation 7). Because of the insecurity of the time and the
fear in the hearts of many people this will be a very fruitful
time for evangelism, and as a result a great number of people
will come to faith:

*'After these things I looked, and behold, a great
multitude which no one could number, of all nations,
tribes, peoples, and tongues, standing before the throne
and before the Lamb, clothed with white robes, with
palm branches in their hands, and crying out with a loud
voice, saying, "Salvation belongs to our God who sits on
the throne, and to the Lamb!"'*

(Revelation 7:9-10)

For the most part these people will be martyred for their faith,
as the persecutions of the Great Tribulation get under way:

*'When He opened the fifth seal, I saw under the altar the
souls of those who had been slain for the word of God
and for the testimony, which they held. And they cried
with a loud voice, saying, "How long, O Lord, holy and
true, until You judge and avenge our blood on those who
dwell on the earth?"'*

(Revelation 6:9-10)

*'Then one of the elders answered, saying to me, "Who
are these arrayed in white robes, and where did they
come from?" And I said to him, "Sir, you know." So he
said to me, "These are the ones who come out of the
great tribulation, and washed their robes and made them
white in the blood of the Lamb."'*

(Revelation 7:13-14)

The majority of people, however, will not turn to Jesus Christ
but to Antichrist. During the first half of the seven-year Great
Tribulation period the Beast or Antichrist is in power, but
not absolutely. During this time he has the backing of the
Babylon world religious system, a coming together of world
faiths to try to save the world from disaster. We have already

seen how global threats to the environment, fear of terrorism and other world crises are bringing nations and religions together in a search for a solution.

During the first half of the Tribulation this Babylon religious system will persecute those who come to believe in Jesus. This religious organisation will support the Antichrist in his rise to absolute power. A point, which is often missed by Bible commentators, is that mid-way through the Tribulation period (i.e. after 3½ years) there is a change in the way things are run by the Antichrist. The one world religious system of Babylon and the 10 kings are the religious and political power base of Antichrist in first half of Tribulation. But mid-way through several things happen. (Note the time period referred to in *Daniel* and *Revelation* – a time, times and half a time = 3½ years (Daniel 7:25); half of seven years = 3½ years (final *'week'* of Daniel 9:27); 42 months = 3½ years (Revelation 13:5); 1260 days = 3½ years (Revelation 12:6).)

At the present time Satan is not seated on a fiery throne in hell with a pitchfork in his hand as he is sometimes colourfully presented. He is the 'prince of the power of the air' ruling over the present evil in the world, from his position between humanity and the throne of God. Before we believe in Jesus, Satan is in a position above us. Therefore he is able to control our thinking. Once we believe in the Lord Jesus the way is open for us to be above him, as we let God control our thinking and our lives. Paul describes this as being seated with Christ in heavenly places, far above Satan's rule (Ephesians 1:15-2:10).

Halfway through the Tribulation Satan is cast out of his present position to the earth (Revelation 12:6-12), when he gives all power to his man on the earth, the Antichrist. This is the point at which the Antichrist has his counterfeit death and resurrection, which causes the world to marvel after him as we saw in the previous chapter. Then the False Prophet sets up the image of the Beast to be worshipped. At this point there is a trinity of evil in control. The dragon (Satan) gives power to his man on earth (the Antichrist), who is borne witness to by the False Prophet. This is a counterfeit of the Father, Son and Holy Spirit. Satan always imitates God, and he wants to take the place of God on earth and be worshipped alone.

For this reason the Beast turns against and eliminates Ecclesiastical Babylon. Not only does he want to prevent people from worshipping the true God through Jesus the Messiah. He wants all worship to be directed to himself. This is shown by a number of scriptures:

> *'Then the king shall do according to his own will: he shall exalt and magnify himself above every god, shall speak blasphemies against the God of gods, and shall prosper till the wrath has been accomplished; for what has been determined shall be done. He shall regard neither the God of his fathers nor the desire of women, nor regard any god; for he shall exalt himself above them all.'*
>
> (Daniel 11:36-7)

> *'Let no one deceive you by any means; for that Day will not come unless the falling away comes first, and the man of sin is revealed, the son of perdition, who opposes and exalts himself above all that is called God or that is worshiped, so that he sits as God in the temple of God, showing himself that he is God.'*
>
> (2 Thessalonians 2:3-4)

> *'These will make war with the Lamb, and the Lamb will overcome them, for He is Lord of lords and King of*

kings; and those who are with Him are called, chosen, and faithful. Then he said to me, "The waters which you saw, where the harlot sits, are peoples, multitudes, nations, and tongues. And the ten horns, which you saw on the beast, these will hate the harlot, make her desolate and naked, eat her flesh and burn her with fire. For God has put it into their hearts to fulfil His purpose, to be of one mind, and to give their kingdom to the beast, until the words of God are fulfilled. And the woman whom you saw is that great city which reigns over the kings of the earth."'

(Revelation 17:14 –18)

Note that in all these passages the Beast turns against all religions, not just on Bible-believing followers of Jesus. His aim is the elimination of all faiths. They will be replaced with a new Messiah who is to be worshipped by all, and who will be empowered by Satan to do counterfeit miracles. Those who reject the Gospel will receive the strong delusion and believe that he is a divine being.

At the end of the Tribulation period, the Lord Jesus will return and personally destroy the world political and religious system of the satanic trinity. This event is described in a number of scriptures, including Daniel 2 where '*the stone*' (representing the Second Coming of the Lord Jesus) strikes the image (representing the world system) and destroys it. The 'stone' then fills the whole earth, which is the event prophesied in Revelation 11:15: *'The kingdoms of this world have become the kingdoms of our Lord and of His Christ and He shall reign forever and ever!'*

The Beast and the False Prophet will be thrown straight into the lake of fire and Satan will be bound for 1000 years, during which time the Lord Jesus will reign on the earth. He will return with the saints who have previously been taken in the Rapture:

> *'Now Enoch, the seventh from Adam, prophesied about these men also, saying, "Behold, the Lord comes with ten thousands of His saints, to execute judgment on all, to convict all who are ungodly among them of all their ungodly deeds which they have committed in an ungodly way, and of all the harsh things which ungodly sinners have spoken against Him."'*

(Jude 14-5)

He will resurrect those who have been put to death by the Antichrist during the Great Tribulation:

> *'Then I saw the souls of those who had been beheaded for their witness to Jesus and for the word of God, who had not worshiped the beast or his image, and had not received his mark on their foreheads or on their hands. And they lived and reigned with Christ for a thousand years.'*

(Revelation 20:4)

He will also resurrect all the saints (true believers) from the Old Testament days:

> *'And many of those who sleep in the dust of the earth shall awake, some to everlasting life, some to shame and everlasting contempt.'*

(Daniel 12:2)

CONCLUSION

Conclusion

14 *Hope for the Future*

||||||||||||||||||||||||||||||||||||||||||||||||||||||||||||||||||||||||||||||||||||||||||||||||||||||||||||||||||||||||

Many people today wonder what is the future of our planet. There is widespread anxiety about the financial situation, the spread of weapons of mass destruction, terrorism, the environment, social disorder, immorality and violence. Any number of world situations could suddenly tip us over into a frightening new crisis, creating chaos and anarchy, or a dictatorial world government with huge technical resources at its disposal to control the population.

Today we see events shaping up in the Middle East, in the world political scene, in the breakdown of moral values and spread of false religion. These tie up with Bible prophecy and are preparing the way for the last days' Tribulation prophesied by the Lord Jesus.

But is there a hope for the future of the earth? As we have already seen, Jesus told the disciples:

'Now when these things (i.e. the signs of his coming) begin to happen, look up and lift up your heads because your redemption draws near.'

(Luke 21:28)

As far as unbelievers are concerned, these things coming on the world are a sign of approaching doom. As far as believers

are concerned, they are a sign of approaching deliverance at
the return of the Lord:

> 'For the Lord Himself will descend from heaven with
> a shout, with the voice of an archangel, and with the
> trumpet of God. And the dead in Christ will rise first.
> Then we who are alive and remain shall be caught up
> to meet the Lord in the air. And thus we shall always be
> with the Lord.'
>
> (1 Thessalonians 4:16-17)

> 'Behold I tell you a mystery: "We shall not all sleep, but
> we shall all be changed – in a moment, in the twinkling
> of an eye, at the last trumpet. For the trumpet will
> sound and the dead will be raised incorruptible, and
> we shall be changed. For this corruptible (body) must
> put on incorruption and this mortal (body) must put
> on immortality."'
>
> (1 Corinthians 15:51-3)

This means that believers have a glorious prospect in front
of them. According to these verses, there is one generation
which will not see death, because they will be alive at the time
of the coming of the Lord. They will experience a marvellous
transformation at the event known as the Rapture, in which
they will receive a new body which will never get sick or old
or die, but will be perfect without spot or blemish. They will
be caught up to meet the Lord in the air as He comes. All
those who died before this event will also be resurrected and
also receive a new body. So all believers will be united with
the Lord at this time.

This glorious future is only available to those who accept
Jesus as Saviour, so if you have not yet done so, now is the
time to take this step.

*'The time is fulfilled, and the kingdom of God is at hand.
Repent and believe the Gospel."*

(Mark 1:15)

*'If you confess with your mouth the Lord Jesus and
believe in your heart that God raised him from the dead,
you will be saved.'*

(Romans 10:9)

The following prayer is an invitation to accept Jesus
as Saviour:

*Dear Heavenly Father, I admit that I am a
sinner and need Your forgiveness. I believe that
Jesus is the Messiah who died in my place,
paying the penalty for my sins. I ask You to
forgive me for all the sins I have committed. I
am willing right now to accept the salvation,
which Jesus gained for me when He died on
the cross and rose again from the dead. I
commit my life to You and ask You to send the
Holy Spirit into my life, to fill me and to guide
me in the way I should go. Please help me to
follow You all the days of my life.*

*Thank You, Father, for loving me. In Jesus'
name, Amen.*

For those who do this, the future is so wonderful that it is
beyond the power of human words to describe or human
minds to comprehend:

*'Eye has not seen, nor ear heard, nor have entered into
the heart of man the things which God has prepared for
those who love him.'*

(1 Corinthians 2:9)

After Jesus has taken us, either in death or the Rapture, we will appear before Him:

> 'For we must all appear before the judgment seat of
> Christ, that each one may receive the things done in
> the body, according to what he has done, whether good
> or bad.'
>
> (2 Corinthians 5:10)

This is not a judgement for heaven or hell, but a judgement of believers for rewards according to what we have done while we were alive. Therefore we need to use the time that remains to us in this life to serve the Lord and to seek to win others to Him.

This will be followed by the glorious reunion described in the *Book of Revelation*, the Marriage of the Lamb:

> 'And I heard as it were the voice of a great multitude,
> as the sound of many waters and as the sound of mighty
> thunderings, saying, "Alleluia! For the Lord God
> Omnipotent reigns! Let us rejoice and give him glory,
> for the marriage of the Lamb has come, and his wife has
> made herself ready." And to her it was granted to be
> arrayed in fine linen, clean and bright, for the fine linen
> represents the righteous acts of the saints. Then he said
> to me, "Write: Blessed are those who are called to the
> marriage supper of the Lamb!"'
>
> (Revelation 19:6-9)

This tremendous event will gather together all those who have trusted the Lord for the greatest celebration, which has ever been known. This meeting takes place *'in the air'* (in other words not on the earth). But the next stage of the programme is the physical return of the Lord Jesus to the earth. He will not come alone but with all the believers with Him:

> *'Then I saw heaven opened and behold a white horse.*
> *And He who sat on him was called Faithful and True,*
> *and in righteousness He judges and makes war. ... He*
> *was clothed with a robe dipped in blood, and His name*
> *is called the Word of God. And the armies in heaven,*
> *clothed in fine linen, white and clean, followed Him on*
> *white horses.'*
>
> (Revelation 19:11-14)

Revelation 19:8 tells us that the *'fine linen represents the righteousness of the saints'* thus identifying this army with the believers in Jesus, as well as the angelic armies which will accompany the Lord. (N.B. In the New Testament the word *'saint'* means anyone who believes in Jesus as Saviour and Lord).

Zechariah 14 is a parallel passage to this and tells us (verse 5) that the Lord will come with the saints at the height of a worldwide conflict over Jerusalem. This event will bring about a swift and sudden end to the satanic trinity:

> *'Now out of his mouth goes a sharp sword, that with it*
> *he should strike the nations. And He Himself will rule*
> *them with a rod of iron. ... And I saw the beast, the kings*
> *of the earth and their armies, gathered together to make*
> *war against him who sat on the horse and against his*
> *army. Then the beast was captured and with him the false*
> *prophet who worked signs in his presence, by which he*
> *deceived those who received the mark of the beast and*
> *worshipped his image. These two were cast alive into the*
> *lake of fire burning with brimstone.'*
>
> (Revelation 19:15, 19-20)

While the Beast and the False Prophet are thrown straight into the lake of fire, the dragon, Satan, is bound in a pit for a thousand years during which time he will be unable to deceive the nations (Revelation 19:20 – 20:3).

The believers who return with the Lord will reign with him in the Messianic Kingdom, or Millennium, which follows. Those who turned to the Lord and refused the mark of the Beast during the Tribulation and were martyred for their faith will then be resurrected and also reign with Christ (Revelation 20:4), along with all Old Testament saints (Daniel 12:2). Those who survive the Tribulation period as believers and do not receive the mark of the Beast will live on in their mortal bodies and have children in the normal way.

During this time God will demonstrate how the earth should be run. After the devastation caused by the Tribulation period, living waters will flow out from Jerusalem to clean up the earth (Zechariah 14:8). Weapons of war will be destroyed and all military training will cease:

'He shall judge between the nations and shall rebuke many people; they shall beat their swords into ploughshares and their spears into pruning hooks. Nation shall not lift up sword against nation, neither shall they learn war any more.'

(Isaiah 2:4)

(See also Isaiah 9:5 and Ezekiel 39:9)

The nations will go up to the redeemed Jerusalem where the Messiah Jesus will teach them the ways of the Lord. There will be universal peace and even the animal kingdom will be affected with meat-eating creatures becoming vegetarian. The earth shall be full of the knowledge of the Lord as the waters cover the sea (Isaiah 11:6-9).

This glorious time will be a Sabbath of rest for the earth. If we take a literal view of creation and reckon the Second Coming of Christ to be not too far away, this gives about 6000 years from creation to the end of this age. The Millennial period will last 1000 years according to Revelation. In 2 Peter 3:8 we read that a day with the Lord is as 1000 years. So we have a parallel with the creation account: six days of labour followed by the Sabbath day of rest; 6000 years of travail and sin on the earth, followed by 1000 years of rest and peace.

In this time, Messiah Jesus will *'rule with a rod of iron'*, but also with absolute justice (Isaiah 11:4-5). The benefits will be obvious to all, especially those who have experienced the horrors of the Great Tribulation. Children will be born during this time in the natural way to survivors of the Great Tribulation who enter the Messianic kingdom. They will not have the opportunity to sin in the way we have today, Satan being bound and unable to influence the nations, and Jesus ruling with power on the earth.

However, the possibility of sin will be present amongst those born during this time. In Isaiah 65:20 we read:

'No more shall an infant from there live but a few days, nor an old man who has not fulfilled his days; for the child shall die one hundred years old, but the sinner being one hundred years old shall be accursed.'

We also read of nations which refuse to worship the Lord during this time and suffer judgment as a result (Zechariah 14:17-19). At the end of the 1000 year period, Satan will be loosed for a while and gather together those have never accepted Jesus as Saviour and Lord and who are inwardly rebelling against His rule. Even after experiencing the good government of the Lord they will demonstrate the depth of human sin by choosing Satan rather then God:

> *'Now when the thousand years have expired, Satan will be released from his prison and will go out to deceive the nations which are in the four corners of the earth, Gog and Magog, to gather them together to battle whose number is as the sand of the sea. They went up on the breadth of the earth and surrounded the camp of the saints and the beloved city. And fire came down from God out of heaven and devoured them. And the devil who deceived them was cast into the lake of fire and brimstone where the beast and the false prophet are. And they will be tormented day and night for ever and ever.'*
>
> (Revelation 20:7-10)

This will actually be the last battle on earth and, like Armageddon, it will end in a moment with Satan's forces being routed. It will also be the end of the world. This earth and everything in it will be destroyed. The final Day of Judgment for those who have rejected the Lord Jesus before the Great White Throne of God will take place.

Zechariah speaks of the Feast of Tabernacles being celebrated during this time. The Feast of Tabernacles is a festival looking back to the time when the Israelites dwelt in booths after they came out of Egypt and before they came into the Promised Land. The booths represent a temporary dwelling place before the final destination, which God has prepared for his people. So the Millennium is a temporary dwelling place for those who have 'come out of Egypt' (symbolising the world system in rebellion against God) before entering into the final rest in heaven.

Revelation 19-21 gives a prophetic overview of the events of the end of the world which follows a logical sequence: the battle of Armageddon, the Second Coming of Christ to the earth, His rule for 1000 years, Satan's loosing and rebellion at the end of the 1000 years, the end of the world, heaven and hell.

After all this the physical universe in its present form will *'melt with fervent heat'* and the earth will be burnt up (2 Peter 3:10). The wicked dead will come before God in judgment:

> *'Then I saw a great white throne and him who sat*
> *on it from whose face the earth and the heaven fled*
> *away. And there was found no place for them. And I*
> *saw the dead, small and great, standing before God,*
> *and books were opened. And another book was opened*
> *which is the Book of Life. And the dead were judged*
> *by their works, by the things, which were written in*
> *the books. The sea gave up the dead who were in it,*
> *and Death and Hades delivered up the dead who were*
> *in them. And they were judged, each one according to*
> *his works. Then Death and Hades were cast into the*
> *lake of fire. This is the second death. And anyone not*
> *found written in the Book of Life was cast into the lake*
> *of fire.'*

(Revelation 20:11-15)

While many try to avoid the subject, the Bible is clear that hell exists. It is a place of absolute separation from God for eternity. Jesus made it clear that nothing is more important than making sure we avoid this place of torment:

> *'Do not be afraid of those who can kill the body, but who*
> *cannot kill the soul. But rather be afraid of the one who*
> *is able to destroy both body and soul in hell.'*

(Matthew 10:28)

People often ask, "How can a loving God send people to hell?" In fact God has done all that He can to save us from hell. According to His justice He must punish sin. In His love and mercy the Lord Jesus left heaven and became man. He lived a perfect life without sin and then endured the punishment we deserve by dying for us on the cross. Being the sinless Son of God, His sacrifice was accepted by the Father. Therefore all who repent (turn from sin) and believe in Jesus as Saviour and Lord are born again of the Holy Spirit, and so receive eternal life.

> *'For God so loved the world that He gave his only begotten Son, that whoever believes in Him should not perish but have everlasting life. ... He who believes in the Son has everlasting life; and he who does not believe the Son shall not see life, but the wrath of God abides on him.'*
>
> (John 3:16, 36)

The Eternal One became the sin offering for the world, both Jew and Gentile, in order that we could be saved from hell for eternity. It is not God who sends people to hell, as much as we who send ourselves there if we refuse to accept the great sacrifice He has made for us.

Those who are saved through putting their trust in Jesus as Saviour and Lord enter into eternal life in heaven. Here at last we will experience eternal deliverance from the troubles and pains of this life. Heaven will not end in failure as all the ages of this world have ended, because of human sinfulness and satanic activity. Only the Lord will be present there and all those who have been redeemed. Satan and those who have rejected this redemption will be unable to enter.

In the presence of the Lord the redeemed will have full, unbroken fellowship with God, which we can never achieve on earth because of the weakness of human nature. We will have new bodies, which will never get old, sick or die (1 Corinthians 15). We will also be recognisable to those who have known us and will preserve our identity. Human relationships will not be on the same basis as on earth. There is no marriage in heaven for example (Luke 20:35-36). Because there is no death there is no need for a new generation to replace the old. But fellowship between the redeemed will be more wonderful than anything we have ever experienced on earth. The bond of love in heaven is stronger than the strongest bonds on earth.

In God's presence is fullness of joy. No one is ever sad in heaven. None of the things that cause unhappiness on earth can enter heaven. There is no unkindness, no cruelty, no selfishness, no loneliness, no misunderstanding, no hatred and no war.

'And God shall wipe away every tear from our eyes; and there shall be no more death, or mourning, or crying or pain.'

(Revelation 1:4)

See you there?

For more details about the author, see page 240.

We hope you enjoyed reading this
New Wine book.
For details of other New Wine books
and a wide range of titles from other
Word and Spirit publishers visit our website:
www.newwineministries.co.uk
or email us at newwine@xalt.co.uk

Tony Pearce produces a quarterly magazine 'Light for the Last Days' which is available on a subscription basis. The magazine covers issues raised in this book – signs of the Second Coming in current events relating to Israel, the world and the church. He also writes a monthly column on 'Signs of the Times' in the Prophetic Witness magazine and produces a monthly talk on the subject 'This month in prophecy,' which is available on CD or online at www. thismonthinprophecy.com

Tony is an elder at The Bridge Christian Fellowship in Golders Green, north London. He is a frequent speaker there and many of his talks are available online at www.bridgelane. org.uk . We also have CDs of his talks.

Other writings by Tony Pearce include: 'The Messiah Factor'. This book looks at issues of Messianic prophecy and answers the questions Jewish people have about Jesus. It shows how the Hebrew prophets point to Jesus as the Messiah of Israel.

'What is the World Heading for?' This is a 28 page booklet giving ten signs of the Second Coming of Christ, which is suitable for giving to non believers. It has been translated into most European languages as well as Hebrew, Arabic and Indian languages.

'The Omega Course.' A booklet giving a self study course on end time prophecy. This booklet is suitable for individual study or groups. There are CDs of talks relating to the topics in the course available.

For information about any of these subjects contact Tony Pearce at:

Light for the Last Days
Box BM–4226
London
WC1N 3XX
www.lightforthelastdays.co.uk